# THE SPIRIT THAT MOVES US

## VOLUME III

USING LITERATURE, ART, AND MUSIC
TO TEACH ABOUT THE HOLOCAUST
AT THE SECONDARY AND COLLEGE LEVEL

by Lorry Stillman
in association with
The Holocaust Human Rights Center of Maine

TILBURY HOUSE PUBLISHERS

GARDINER, MAINE

## TILBURY HOUSE, PUBLISHERS

2 Mechanic Street
Gardiner, Maine 04345
800-582-1899
www.tilburyhouse.com

**Design & Layout**   Rosemary Giebfried, Bangor, ME
**Editorial & Production**   Jennifer Elliott
Barbara Diamond
**Printing & Binding**   Graphic Services, Rockland, MA

☐

10 9 8 7 6 5 4 3 2 1

☐

☐

This guide is dedicated to
Maine Holocaust survivors and their families,

and the educators
who will continue to tell their stories.

The writing of this volume was made possible, in part,
by generous grants from
The Simmons Foundation
and the
Dorothy Levine Alfond Endowment Fund.

# Contents

## POETRY OF THE HOLOCAUST

## ART: BEFORE, DURING, AND AFTER WW II

## MUSIC OF THE HOLOCAUST

# Preface

As a child, I spent my summers with my family at a local beach resort. My days were filled with the unfamiliar accents of the vacationing Jewish families staying in the boardinghouse next to ours. I grew up in the kosher kitchens of this house sampling the rich potato puddings and reveling in the animated evening discussions on the porch. The mothers and fathers spoke a lively Yiddish punctuated with American slang. But the curious numbers tattooed on their forearms and the anxious protectiveness over their children when swimming at the seaside led me to question my mother about their background. My mother replied simply that they were from far away and had been through hard times.

This was the extent of my knowledge of these European refugees of the pogroms, concentration camps, and death camps of Eastern Europe. The word "Holocaust" was an unfamiliar term in our Orthodox Jewish home, and although many of the members of my synagogue also spoke in foreign accents, I knew nothing about the terrors they had survived and the hardships they had endured. Holocaust education was not a part of the curriculum of the small elementary yeshiva I attended. I read *The Diary of Anne Frank* as a teenager and identified only with her adolescent conflicts with her mother. I simply did not know that there had been a man named Hitler who had systematically murdered approximately six million Jews and changed the world in incomprehensible ways.

Holocaust education came to me late in my college years. I became familiar with world history and literature and began to understand the full meaning of the Holocaust of World War II. Yet, it was not until I read Elie Wiesel's *Night* in a contemporary novel class that my perspective on literature and education was forever changed. I slowly began my journey into this image-rich world of human suffering, and my career as an English teacher has reinforced my very strong belief in Holocaust education.

Holocaust literature, art, and music are guides to the most important ideas we can share with our students. The artistic imagery of the writers, artists, and musicians of those times teaches us to understand the horror of the Holocaust as an archetypal experience. Personal testimony gives voice to hope, honor, and courage. Art and music provide meaningful expressions of emotion, giving validation to diverse methods of seeing and learning. Experiences are expressed for students in metaphoric language, enlarging their perspective on the human condition. The emotions of care and responsibility coupled with moral and ethical values begin the discussions on social action, community responsibility, and personal culpability.

The experience of teaching a Holocaust class has enriched me both as a teacher and a member of a larger community. In my classes, the students express and share their outrage and confusion about the historical events we study. I listen to their earnest voices discussing ethical and moral issues as they search for answers to difficult questions. They explore their roles as responsible members of a community as they write poignantly about their families and friends. We share our fears and hopes for the future. We all gain an appreciation of the similarities and differences among us. Together we learn to express ourselves respectfully, and we listen sympathetically.

This resource guide on the Holocaust gives teachers multiple opportunities to bring Holocaust education to the students in their classes. It reinforces the importance of teaching our students about diversity, prejudice, and tolerance. The guide contains materials that encourage students to become aware of the changing face of our world while still showing respect and honor for the past. Written with a focus on interdisciplinary education, the guide will help teachers of language arts, history, art, music, and the humanities find ideas for single-unit assignments or for longer, more fully developed courses. Education about World War II and the Holocaust is a map our students can use as they move into the world beyond their schools. They will have the tools to become the generation to bear witness with a conviction to promote change and understanding.

In an assignment I give to my Holocaust literature students, I ask them to write a Bill of Rights for Children. They bring me their slips of paper expressing the simplest and most profound demands: Children should be at peace, loved, nourished emotionally and physically, educated; they should play and experience joy; and, most importantly, children should feel safe. These are the lessons of life illuminated by the testimonies and stories of the Holocaust. They are more than the lessons of tragedy; they are the lessons of community and family values and behavior. It is crucial that educators and students share these lessons.

My journey in understanding the lessons of the Holocaust began as I listened to the laughter and joy of a group of immigrants celebrating life at a seaside resort. These families understood the importance of their memories and the promise of the future. I have learned from them to appreciate the simple pleasures of a life of family, friends, and study. I am grateful to my husband and children who have helped me to understand and appreciate this joy in living. Their patience and love have been the primary resource for this guide.

—Lorry Stillman
Portland, Maine

# Acknowledgments _____

The dedicated efforts of the members of the Holocaust Human Rights Center of Maine and its education committee have been essential in creating *The Spirit That Moves Us*, Volume III.

I would like to thank Ragnhild Baade, Robert Katz, George Lyons, Winnie McPhedran, Cathy Wimett, J. Gary Nichols, Nancy Schatz, Donna Taranko, Linda Voss, Cecelia E. Levine, Gail Lamb, Jennifer Denis, Alison Mizner, Steve Hochstadt, Jean M. Peck, Jennifer Elliott, and Barbara Diamond for their work reviewing and editing the guide.

I am grateful to Sharon Nichols for her patience and guidance throughout the entire project, and I extend my appreciation to Sue Stein for her masterful editing skills.

To my husband Neal, and children Jessica and Robert: your support and encouragement have made this all possible.

Thank you.

# Introduction

## Why Study the Holocaust?

> The principle of art is to pause, not bypass. The principles of true art is not to portray, but to evoke. This requires a moment of pause—a contract with yourself through the object you look at or the page you read. In that moment of pause, I think life expands. And really the purpose of art—for me, of fiction—is to alert, to indicate to stop, to say: Make sure that when you rush through you will not miss the moment which you might have had, or might still have. That is the moment of something that you have not known about yourself, or your environment, about others and about life.[1]

> Jerzy Kosinski

This quote expresses a truly significant idea to the modern world: to pause. The study of the Holocaust and the events of World War II provide opportunities for both teachers and students alike to suspend time and reflect upon the past, present, and future history of our world. It is a pause in our busy daily lives in which to ask questions, find our voices, and learn to react appropriately to new ideas and feelings.

Each fall when I teach my high-school students a course on literature of the Holocaust, I pause. My lesson plans abandon the frantic pace of a school semester as we take the time to read, write, and discuss. We ponder questions beyond the classroom and reflect on the experiences of the Holocaust in relationship to current political and social events. We learn to respect each other's feelings and express concern and confusion in articulate and patient voices. And we pause to remember that what has occurred in history affects our personal lives. The study of the Holocaust allows us to "not rush through," to "not miss the moment."

The Holocaust was an aggressive campaign by the Nazi Party of Germany during World War II to eliminate the population of Jews throughout Europe. Under the leadership of Adolf Hitler, the Nazis designed and organized a system of torture and death in concentration camps and death camps. Approximately 6 million innocent Jewish men, women, and children, as well as millions of non-combatants, were murdered. The study of this terrible time in history allows students to learn about and recognize the elements of persecution and power that reigned in the Third Reich. Study of the Holocaust teaches students about human suffering and triumph over evil. It encourages discussion about prejudice and justice, shame and dignity, hopelessness and faith. Holocaust study involves students in debate about the moral and ethical behavior of humankind.

High-school students are impressionable and forceful in their opinions and ideas. Holocaust study provides a model for understanding diversity and acceptance. As the face of America changes, children must learn to look with accepting and respectful eyes at the differences in race and religion. Holocaust study gives perspective to stereotyping and peer pressure. The reading of literature and the study of the visual and performing arts helps to develop a personal identification with the peoples of the world. Students learn about care and compassion. They begin to understand what their part is in forming a diverse community. By talking, debating, and writing, students learn to find their true and honest voices and to listen to the voices around them. Students see the clear connections between themselves and characters in literature. Study of the Holocaust brings us together in our pursuit of equality and freedom for all.

Literature, art, and music are important tools with which to articulate memory, experience, and emotion. The use of narrative fiction, non-fiction, music, and visual art allows students to hear a narrative voice recount not only the fact but also the emotion of history. The study of personal testimony and fiction helps to make connections to the past and provides a map for the future. André Wat said,

> You must touch the reader because the reader will not be touched by history on its own. In your stories, you must recreate the state of oppression that is present in the stories you tell. And remember, you will not be able to use gestures, nobody will hear your accent; they will not see your eyes or the agony you express with your body language, everything must be contained in the verbs, adjectives, nouns, and adverbs. [2]

Literature and art develop a student's ability to recognize archetypal symbols, imagery, description, detail, mood, tone, and style. Holocaust literature and art promote the imagination of students, freeing them to experiment with ideas and creative means of self-expression. And the study of language gives students the opportunity to experiment with their own voices, a means to experiment with personal artistry, not just a distant historical event.

Perhaps the most important aspect of Holocaust study is the promotion of questions by our students. Students begin to find answers to questions about silence, complicity, moral and ethical choices, responsibility, and action. The study of the fiction and personal testimony of Holocaust survivors creates a forum for students to begin to examine their roles in the worldwide community.

## The Purpose of the Guide

The Holocaust Human Rights Center of Maine is committed to the study of social justice, diversity, and Holocaust education. This third guide is designed for teachers of high-school and college-level students. It provides extensive literary and artistic analysis of the personal testimony, fiction, poetry, short stories, art, and music of the Holocaust. The guide contains a select bibliography of research sources, glossaries, character lists, and suggested reading lists for teachers and students. All chapters have a brief plot summary of the piece of literature. The chapters include an analysis of symbol, imagery, language, and style and their roles in developing a historical understanding of the Holocaust years. A list of documentary and artistic films is also included.

The lesson plans and suggestions for writing and research projects are designed to reach all levels of academic study. It is possible for each suggested writing and research idea to be modified or enlarged, depending on the level of instruction. For example, an extensive, written autobiography can be supplemented with a short personal essay, a collage, a video, or a dramatic presentation. The level of literary analysis can be as extensive as teachers desire, from focusing on the plot and historical significance of a piece of literature to the more developed study of literature and art as symbol, metaphor, and artistic documentation of historical experience.

The novels and personal testimonies outlined in the guide vary in length. Recognizing the time constraints of a literature or humanities class, it is suggested that the longer pieces of literature be assigned as summer reading. Whether teaching the selections in this guide as a full-semester class or a single unit on the Holocaust, teachers should consider an interdisciplinary approach. Integrating the materials from the various chapters is helpful in the completion of the novels and testimonies. For example, teachers could assign larger blocks of reading over a period of time, using class discussion for the art and music chapters. Poetry is an important supplement for a literary discussion, and discussion of the novels should be alternated with poetry study. Class projects give students time to complete the reading for homework that allows discussion on more extensive portions of the books.

The resource guides for teachers *The Spirit that Moves Us*, Volumes I and II, seek to provide teachers with a foundation for teaching Holocaust units in the classrooms. The first and second guides, for K–4 and 5–8 respectively, offer reading selections, writing and research ideas, and classroom activities for interdisciplinary study on race, religion, culture, and personal and political freedoms. All of the guides are fully developed resources with glossaries, bibliographies, Internet listings, and suggested reading lists for teachers and students. The materials in the guides are interchangeable, and the Holocaust Human Rights Center of Maine suggests teachers examine all three guides for teaching ideas.

## Objectives for the Use of the Guide
▶ To provide a working curriculum for study of the Holocaust in a high-school or college classroom
▶ To provide historical documentation of the events of World War II
▶ To improve students' understanding of racial prejudice and cultural and religious diversity
▶ To introduce art, music, and literature as forms of expressing metaphor
▶ To encourage and instruct good reading-comprehension skills
▶ To encourage both creative and expository writing

►To teach research and oral-presentation skills

►To encourage small-group work

►To experience reflective-participation and listening skills

►To think critically about human nature and encourage discussion on moral and ethical behaviors

## An Overview of the Guide

The following is an overview of the contents of the guide. The summaries will help teachers decide which materials are appropriate for their classes. The chapters are arranged in a chronological sequence starting with pre-war events and ending in postwar experiences.

The Introduction provides teachers with an overview of the contents of the guide, suggestions on using it, and tools for teaching journal keeping, small-group work, and evaluating presentations. The Introduction also includes a list of Internet resources and a Holocaust Chronology. The Glossary of Terms Used in Holocaust Study gives teachers and students an early working vocabulary of the terms of the Holocaust. Several of the chapters contain their own glossaries pertinent to the subject matter.

The chapters on *Seed of Sarah*, by Judith Isaacson, and *Night*, by Elie Wiesel, focus on the significance of personal testimony. Each chapter examines the historical significance of the events of the text and analyzes the writing style and voice of the survivor. Accompanying the chapters are clear objectives for teaching, analysis of the text, writing and presentation ideas, and a suggested reading list.

The guide also provides a focus on fictional literature of the Holocaust. The chapters on Short Stories, and on the novels *Stones from the River*, by Ursula Hegi, *This Way for the Gas, Ladies and Gentlemen*, by Tadeuz Borowski, *The Shawl* and *Rosa*, by Cynthia Ozick, *Maus*, by Art Spiegelman, and the Poetry chapter examine the role of metaphor and imagery in Holocaust literature. The chapter on *If Not Now, When?* by Primo Levi begins with an introduction on the Jewish resistance movement in Europe. Each chapter analyzes the artistic voice of fiction in depicting historical events. The chapters include objectives for teaching the novels, character lists, glossaries, analysis, writing and presentation ideas, and suggested reading lists.

Continuing with the themes of artistic expression, the chapters on Art: Before, During and After WW II and Music of the Holocaust study the role of the visual and performing arts in Holocaust history. The chapters include examples of artwork and a list of recordings of Holocaust music. Each chapter contains writing and presentation ideas and a suggested reading list.

Also provided in the guide is a list of Supplemental Activities for students. These ideas focus primarily on interdisciplinary research and current events.

The guide has an extensive Bibliography for teachers and students. These titles are useful for research by both students and teachers. It is recommended teachers consult *The Spirit That Moves Us*, Volumes I and II, to complement their lesson planning.

## Teaching Tools

The guide uses several methods of teaching to encourage diversity in the presentation of materials. Holocaust study provides rich opportunities for small-group work, class discussion, journal writing, oral presentation, and artwork. The following are some suggestions for instruction.

### Keeping a Reading-Response Journal

Many chapters of this guide recommend students keep a reading journal. A reading journal provides students a place to articulate their ideas about the literature before they come to class. It is a secure and private place to express emotions, questions, and concerns. Reading journals can also be used in a more controlled manner. Students can use a journal to respond to questions about the literature, writing ideas, and short in-class writing prompts. Students can write their poetry assignments, personal reflections, and vocabulary definitions in their journals. Keeping these writings in a journal enables students to go back and read their own work, reflect upon it, share it with the class, or use it as a resource for creative and research ideas. Evaluation of journals should be based on completion of assignments and depth of written work.

A guide for a reading journal written for distribution to students can be found on **page 14.**

### Tools for Teaching Small-Group Work

Two different models can be used to assign groups. One is to let students decide which topics interest them the most and then group together like-minded students. Students are then invested in the work and share the experience with others who are equally involved. Some negotiations might be needed to make sure each topic of research is covered.

Another method is for teachers to assign the groups. This insures a variety of work skills and personalities. By assigning groups, the teacher can also encourage diversity in student relationships. When assigning the groups, it is always best to give specific tasks to each student. These tasks can be rotated in each group. With four in a group, the following roles can be assigned:

**The leader.** It is the responsibility of the leader to organize each work session. In the first five minutes together, the leader should discuss with the group what the expectations and goals for the work time are. The leader should assign tasks to each student. For example, one student might be using the Internet, two might be researching periodicals, another working on visual props. At the end of each session, the leader should again assess what progress has been made and what the homework or goals for the next class will be.

**The recorder.** It is the responsibility of this student to record the work of the group. Each day the group meets, this student should record the following:

▶ The recorder should note what has been completed in previous sessions or homework assignments.

▶ Goals and expectations for the work session should be discussed and recorded.

▶ The individual tasks of each student should be noted.

▶ Assessment of what was accomplished during the work session should be recorded at the end of the class.

▶ Homework or goals for the next work session should be clearly written down in the recorder's notes.

The form on **page 15** can be used to facilitate the recorder's notes. Teachers can use these sheets to meet with individuals and the group to assess progress, concerns, and questions. The quality of the review sheets should be part of the assessment of the project.

### Class Presentations

Class presentations by either individuals or groups can be a stimulating way for students to learn important information. Specific expectations of a presentation help students to present their projects in the most effective manner. The following are some suggestions for goals and expectations:

▶ Students should meet with the teacher to be sure they understand the assignment. In this session, a statement of purpose should be presented to the teacher explaining what topic the student(s) will be researching.

▶ A specific use of sources provided by the teacher should explain what resources the students are required to use: Internet, encyclopedias, periodicals, fiction, non-fiction. Students should keep a bibliography of all resources.

▶ Various types of presentation methods, oral, written, or visual should be presented to the class. Teachers should be clear about expectations of presentation form: reading, note cards, maps, visual effects, and video. Time allotment for presentations is also an essential directive.

Assessment of research presentations can then be based on the completion of these expectations and the quality of the work. Teachers may also decide to give a grade for process as well as product. The Evaluation Form on **page 16** can be used for teacher and peer assessment.

### Internet Sources

The Internet is a valuable research guide for both students and teachers alike. It contains historical data, maps, audio and visual information, and resources for research, personal testimony, and analysis of the events of the Holocaust. Since there are a number of sites that may be inappropriate for students, it is important for teachers to monitor use of the Internet. Revisionists, neo-Nazi propaganda, and other materials sponsored by hate groups can mislead and misinform students. The following are several Internet sites that support scholarly and informative Holocaust study:

**The United States Holocaust Memorial Museum**

www.ushmm.org

*This site provides a complete description of the museum. It also contains information for teachers on instruction of the Holocaust.*

### The Simon Wiesenthal Center and the Museum of Tolerance

www.wiesenthal.com

*The Museum of Tolerance provides important information on the dynamics of racism and prejudice in America. It also has a number of resources on the history of the Holocaust.*

### The Cybrary of the Holocaust

www.remember.org

*The Cybrary uses art, poetry, discussion groups, photos, and video to provide information on the Holocaust.*

### A Teacher's Guide to the Holocaust

http://fcit.coedu.usf.edu/holocaust

*A Teacher's Guide to the Holocaust is a comprehensive collection of information on the Holocaust.*

### Fortunoff Video Archive for Holocaust Testimonies

www.library.yale.edu/testimonies/homepage.html

*The Fortunoff site provides excerpts from the text of personal testimonies of survivors along with audio and video.*

### Association of Holocaust Organizations

www.ahoinfo.org

*This site provides information about Holocaust centers around the world.*

### Holocaust Education Foundation, Inc.

www.Holocaust-trc.org

*This site provides numerous lesson plans and curricula for educators.*

### Yad Vashem

www.yad-vashem.org.il

*This is the official web site of Israel's Holocaust memorial. The site includes FAQ, a bibliography, and a section on Righteous Among Nations, those who are recognized for helping Jews during the Holocaust.*

### The Anne Frank Center, USA, Inc.

www.annefrank.com

*This site provides information for students and teachers about Anne Frank, along with a virtual tour of Anne Frank's home.*

### The Holocaust Chronicle

www.holocaustchronicle.org

*This site contains every word and image that is in its print edition.*

---

[1] Jerzy Kosinski, *Passing By: Selected Essays 1962–1991.* (Random House Inc., 1992), inscription page.

[2] Ibid., "To Touch Minds," p. 33.

# Chronology of the Holocaust 1933-1945

## 1933

| | |
|---|---|
| **Jan 30** | Adolf Hitler named chancellor of Germany |
| **Mar–July** | One-party Nazi dictatorship established in Germany |
| **Apr 1** | Nazis urge boycott of all Jewish businesses |

## 1935

| | |
|---|---|
| **May 31** | Jews prohibited from serving in German armed forces |
| **Sept 15** | Nuremberg laws strip German Jews of citizenship |

## 1936

| | |
|---|---|
| **May 3** | Jewish doctors barred from German institutions |
| **June 17** | Himmler appointed Chief of Police |

## 1938

| | |
|---|---|
| **Mar 13** | Austria annexed by Germany |
| **July** | Representatives from 32 countries meet at Evian-les-Bains, France, to discuss immigration |
| **Nov 9–10** | Kristallnacht, night of broken glass—Jewish synagogues, stores destroyed; 30,000 Jewish men arrested |
| **Nov 15** | All Jewish children expelled from German schools |

## 1939

| | |
|---|---|
| **Mar 15** | Germany invades Czechoslovakia |
| **Sept 1** | Nazi Germany attacks Poland, beginning World War II. |
| **Sept–Dec** | Polish Jews from areas annexed to Germany expelled to central Poland |
| **Oct–Nov** | First ghettos established in Poland; Polish Jews must wear yellow Star of David |

## 1940

| | |
|---|---|
| **Jan** | Start of "euthanasia program": mental patients killed with poison gas in Germany |
| **Apr–June** | Germany invades and defeats Denmark, Norway, Belgium, Holland, France |
| **May 22** | Creation of Auschwitz concentration camp in Poland |
| **Nov 15** | Warsaw ghetto closed off, largest Polish ghetto with 500,000 Jews |

## 1941

| | |
|---|---|
| **June 22** | Nazi Germany invades Soviet Union; mobile army killing units, called *Einsatzgruppen*, begin mass murder of Soviet Jews by shooting |
| **July 31** | Nazi leaders ordered to formulate a "comprehensive solution to Jewish question" |
| **Sept** | First experimental gassings of Soviet POW's at Auschwitz |
| **Sept 29–30** | Mass murder of Jews at Babi Yar, near Kiev, Ukraine |
| **Dec** | Gassing of Jews and Gypsies begins at Chelmno |

## 1942

| | |
|---|---|
| **Jan 20** | Wannsee Conference of Nazi leaders in Berlin outlines measures to murder Europe's Jews, called "Final Solution" |
| **Mar–July** | Mass murders of Jews in gas chambers begin at death camps in Poland: Belzec, Treblinka, Sobibor, Auschwitz; start of deportations of Dutch and French Jews to Auschwitz and of Warsaw Jews to Treblinka |
| **Sept** | Start of mass gassings at Majdanek |
| **Dec** | Gypsies ordered sent to Auschwitz |

## 1943

| | |
|---|---|
| **Mar** | Start of deportations of Greek Jews to Auschwitz |
| **Apr–May** | Warsaw ghetto revolt by Polish Jews |
| **June** | Nazis order killing of Jews in Polish and Russian ghettos |
| **Aug 2** | Jewish prisoners revolt at Treblinka |
| **Sept** | 7,500 Danish Jews rescued to Sweden |

## 1943 (continued)

| | |
|---|---|
| **Oct 14** | Jewish prisoners revolt at Sobibor |
| **Oct 19** | Death camps at Treblinka, Belzec, Sobibor, Majdanek closed |

## 1944

| | |
|---|---|
| **Apr** | Start of deportations of Hungarian Jews to Auschwitz |
| **July–Dec** | Transports and death marches evacuate Auschwitz |
| **Aug** | Lodz, the last ghetto, liquidated |
| **Oct 7** | Revolt by Jewish *Sonderkommando* in Auschwitz |
| **Nov** | Nazis order end of gassings at Auschwitz |

## 1945

| | |
|---|---|
| **Jan 27** | Soviet troops liberate Auschwitz |
| **Apr–May** | Allied troops liberate camps in Germany |
| **May 7** | Nazi Germany surrenders |
| **November** | War Crimes Tribunal established at Nuremberg |

*Chronology by Steve Hochstadt, Ph.D., History Department, Bates College*

**Anschluss.** Incorporation of Austria by the Germans

**Aryan.** Originally, the language spoken by Indo-European people; term characterized by the Nazis: the "race" of Germans "superior" to all other races

**Concentration Camps.** Prisons for political prisoners, religious dissidents, and "non-Aryan" people; by the end of World War II, the Germans had established more than one hundred major camps

**Displaced Persons Camp.** Camps set up after WW II by the Allies to house Holocaust survivors and other refugees

**Final Solution.** The Nazi code name for the physical extermination of the Jews; the term was first penned at the Wannsee Conference of 1942 where the coordination and implementation of the plan was designed

**Führer.** The title used by Hitler; German word for leader

**Gas Chambers.** Rooms at the killing centers that were sealed; the poisonous gas Zyklon B was released, killing prisoners within

**Genocide.** The systematic killing of a nation or race of people

**Gestapo.** Secret German police during Nazi regime

**Ghetto.** A medieval term originally designating an urban district where Jews were required to live; used during World War II by the Germans to label the "compulsory Jewish Quarters"[2] in a city or town; ghettos were surrounded by walls and barbed wire restricting the entrance and departure of the Jews within their confines

**Holocaust.** From the Greek meaning *"burnt whole"*; the systematic extermination of European Jews and non-Jews during WW II

**Imagery.** Literary or artistic expression with rich and complex details of ideas, objects, and feelings

**Juden.** German for Jews

**Judenrat.** Jewish Council of Elders

**Kaddish.** Jewish prayer for the dead

**Kapo.** From the Latin "capo" meaning "head"; a term used in the concentration camps and death camps to designate inmates who worked as functionaries of the camp; the kapos oversaw work detail and daily rituals of their fellow inmates and received privileges for their compliance with the Nazis

**Killing Centers.** Camps built by the Germans for mass extermination: Auschwitz, Belzec, Chelmno, Majdanek, Sobibor, and Treblinka

**Kristallnacht.** "Night of Broken Glass," a pogrom initiated on the nights of November 9–10, 1938, by the German Propaganda Minister Joseph Goebbels; three hundred synagogues destroyed; thousands of Jewish-owned businesses destroyed; one hundred Jews killed; the signaling event for the start of the Holocaust

**Labor Camp.** A concentration camp in which prisoners were used as forced laborers

**Liberators.** Soldiers who freed the survivors of the concentration camps

**Lodz.** City in Poland where the first major ghetto was established

**Musselmänner.** A term for the prisoners who, as a result of exhaustion and starvation, stopped fighting for survival

**Nuremberg Laws.** Laws issued in 1935 by the German government to further the legal exclusion of Jews from German life

**Nuremberg Trial.** Trial of Nazi war criminals in 1945–46

**Partisans.** Guerrilla fighters, resistance fighters

**Prejudice.** An opinion formed before the facts are known, based on rumors, myth, ignorance, lies, and fear

**Resettlement.** A German euphemism for deportation

**Resistance Movement.** Groups organized to resist, sabotage, and defeat the Nazis

**Righteous Gentiles.** Christians who risked their lives to save Jews during the Holocaust

**SS.** Members of Hitler's elite force of stormtroopers

**Scapegoat.** A person or group who is made the object of blame for the mistakes or crimes of others

**Shoah.** Hebrew word for remembrance

**Survivors.** Persons who survived the Nazi persecution from 1933–45

**Synagogue.** Jewish house of worship

**Third Reich.** Empire of the Nazi Party led by Hitler

**Wannsee Conference.** January 1942 assembly of the powers of the Nazi Party; term "Final Solution" designated there (see Final Solution)

**Warsaw Ghetto.** Established in 1940, where a revolt took place in 1943

**Weimar Republic.** The German Republic 1919–33

**The White Rose.** Small group of students at the University of Munich, led by Hans Scholl and his sister Sophie, who participated in active protests against the Nazis

**Yellow Star.** Forced to be worn by all Jews; the badge used by the Nazis for identification in the occupied countries during World War II; a six-cornered yellow star with the word "Jude" or "Jew" written across it

**Zionism.** Political and cultural movement calling for the return of Jews to Palestine

**Zyklon B.** Hydrogen cyanide, the gas used at the killing centers to exterminate Jews

(See individual chapters for further glossaries.)

---

[1] *Fifty Years Ago: Revolt Amid the Darkness, 1993 Days of Remembrance*, United States Holocaust Memorial Museum, pp. 396–409.

[2] Ibid., p. 400.

# Reading Response Journal

**A response journal** *is a collection of writings you make over the course of study on the Holocaust. It will reflect your ideas, opinions, questions, and concerns about the reading, class discussions, speakers, and presentations.*

*One entry in your journal should accompany each short story, and five to six entries should be made for each novel and personal testimony.*

*Predominantly, you should write your reaction to the reading and class discussions.*

## Questions to answer with each journal entry:

▶ What are your *feelings* about the subject matter?

▶ Do you *identify* in any way with the events of the stories and the lives of the characters?

▶ Do you *sympathize* with any of the characters? Are they realistically developed? Do you understand the joy, sorrow, anger, fear, and shock expressed in the novels and personal testimonies?

▶ Write: It makes me angry when. . . .

▶ Write: It makes me glad when. . . .

▶ Consider world events today. Do you see *similarities? Differences?*

▶ How do the ideas of *tolerance* and *diversity* affect your everyday life at school? At home?

▶ Do you have any questions or concerns?

# Recorder's Notes for Small-Group Work

## 1. Review
▶ Work completed in previous sessions or homework assignments:

## 2. Goals
▶ List goals and expectations for this work session:

## 3. Assignments
▶ List each student's task (i.e., Internet use, researching periodicals, working on visual props):

## 4. Assessment
▶ What was accomplished during this work session?

## 5. Homework
▶ Specify homework or goals for next work session:

## 5. Notes
▶ Additional notes and questions:

# Evaluation Form for Research Presentations

## 1. Process
▶ Use of class time, homework, research methods    5    4    3    2    1

*Comments:*

## 2. Sources
▶ Presented list of resource bibliography    5    4    3    2    1

*Comments:*

## 3. Presentation
▶ Reading, use of note cards, voice    5    4    3    2    1

*Comments:*

## 4. Visual Aids
▶ Video, artwork, maps, charts    5    4    3    2    1

*Comments:*

## 5. Content
▶    5    4    3    2    1

*Comments:*

# Short Stories _____

Short stories are an excellent way to begin a unit on the study of the Holocaust. The brevity of the stories allows for a gradual introduction to the ideas and feelings that surround Holocaust study. The development of characters, setting, and conflict is limited, allowing a wide range of reading levels to engage in the difficult thematic analysis of the pieces.

The following short stories are an excellent means of introducing background information about the Holocaust. This collection of stories allows teachers an opportunity to investigate with the class the historical events of this time in Eastern Europe. The stories take the reader through the early rise to power of the Nazi Party, the enforcement of the Nuremberg Laws, and the eventual roundup, deportation, and murder of the Jews of occupied Europe.

It is important to provide an understanding of this background information before students delve into the complexities of the novels and personal testimonies.

## "The Last of the Just," André Schwarz-Bart

*Out of the Whirlwind: A Reader of Holocaust Literature.* Albert H. Friedlander, ed. (New York: Schocken Books), 1976. ISBN 0-8052-0925-5.

### Character List
> Ernie Levy
> Herr Geek
> Simon Kotkowski
> Moses Finkelstein
> Marcus Rosenberg
> Hans Schliemann
> Ilse

### Plot Summary

This story provides the reader with information about the early days of the Nazi Party. "The Last of the Just" depicts a classroom in Nazi Germany in the 1930s led by a cruel and abusive teacher. Using a child's eye view, Schwarz-Bart illustrates the violence and cruelty imposed upon Jewish children by both adults and children. It is a story of the awakening of an innocent young boy to the horrors of the rule of the Nazis.

The title of this story by André Schwarz-Bart is a biblical reference to a story of thirty-six righteous men saved from the destruction of the world by God. These thirty-six men are from the Israeli tribe of the Levites, and their legacy is to forever hold within them the sins and suffering of the world. Schwarz-Bart uses this Talmudic lesson to create the character Ernie Levy. Young Ernie suffers the injustices of the Nazis and must struggle with this role as a "just man."

### Objectives for Teaching "The Last of the Just"

This story gives unusual insight into the machine of the Nazi Party. In teaching this story, teachers should focus on the following ideas:

▶ Historical documentation of the restrictions on Jews by the Nazi Party
▶ Use of metaphor and imagery to create historical documentation of the early days of Nazism
▶ Psychological study of the young boys and the teacher

### Analysis

The author uses meticulous descriptive detail and narrative voice to create the characters of this story. Herr Geek is introduced as a prototype for a noncommissioned officer of the Nazi Party. His physical description and demeanor create a character of extremes: he is a strong nationalist, a common man who has risen to power by his fervent loyalty, and a brutal tyrant who abuses children. With the use of poetic narrative, Schwarz-Bart defines Geek: "The thin lips stretched like leather thongs opened on a blackened mouth, and the words that escaped from them were as if carved from some hard material, from wood—and brutally, by a machete."[1] This image of stone and carving develops later in the story as a symbol of violence and murder. There is no elegance to this man—just cruel and despotic behavior.

The narrative describes Herr Geek's admonishments to the class and the behavior of the boys. Students should read page 87 to hear the voice of the Nazi Party in its direct assault on the Jews of Eastern Europe. Such terms as "Jewified," "drops of Jewish blood," "hour of the Jews," "victory bell," and "grandeur of the Fatherland" are all reminiscent of the dogma and propaganda delivered to the German people by Hitler.[2] This extreme sense of nationalism is reiterated in the boys' behavior in and out of the classroom. Their behavior is dangerous, and their power is infectious. Led by the ultimate promise, "On that day . . . you will all be men," the boys join Herr Geek in his brutality.[3] They are lured by peer pressure, the promise of the future, and the desire for power and control over their peers. Close study of this story allows for a deeper examination of the effects of Nazism on Germany's youth.

The scene in the classroom also provides keen insight into the classification process Germans used to label Jews. The Nazis devised a "typological" standard for

Jewry involving the measurements of noses, foreheads, lips, and other body parts. Using Darwin's Theory of Evolution, Hitler adopted "bio-political" standards for Aryans and Jews. According to the Nazis, the physical makeup of Jews prevented their race from multiplying. Students should read carefully pages 87–88 for the literary depiction of these theories.

Using Herr Geek's command to sing, Schwarz-Bart gives us a view into the torment and anguish of a Jewish boy during this time. Each Jewish boy assaulted symbolizes a different reaction to the horrors of the Nazis. Simon Kotkowski represents the voice of innocence. He launches into song unaware of the humiliation of singing a death march for Jews. His naiveté defies the Nazi rule for victimization, and as Geek beats him to his knees, the reader witnesses innocence stolen from children. The character Moses Finkelstein sings a voice of complete defeat. Bathed in his own tears, and already an outcast in the classroom, he is beaten for his shame and capitulation. Through Marcus Rosenberg the reader hears the voice of defiance. He refuses to sing, and when forced, "his mouth was wide open, a sudden drowned scream of music escaped it. The proof of Jewish ignominy was proved." [4]

The study of Ernie's response to this series of events is the heart of the story. With his declaration, "I don't know yet if I ought to [sing]," [5] Ernie catapults the reader into his world of confusion and anguish. His response is neither cowardice nor defiance, but moral uncertainty, a behavior that diminishes the ability of Geek to humiliate Ernie. With the arm twisting by Geek, "Ernie had taken his final stand." [6] His lack of singing places him outside the voice of protest or defeat. He becomes the voice of moral right and wrong. He upholds his legacy to share the burden of suffering as a "Just Man," and Ernie escapes to the "height of a dove, crowned by the faces he could not assassinate in song"—his family, the Jewish people. [7] He has become one of the "just" who bears the burden of sin.

The physical beating and emotional humiliation Ernie suffers at the hands of the boys and Ilse is described in a stream of consciousness that parallels the pacing of the acts in destroying Ernie's persona. Losing voice now becomes a physical image of Ernie's despair, and as the boys taunt and assault him, Ernie descends into a world within himself. Students should read the passages on pages 94–96 to hear this style of writing. Schwarz-Bart juxtaposes light and dark, noise and silence, and supreme pain and paralysis against the confusion and disillusionment of Ernie. As the boys uncover Ernie's private parts to view his circumcision, "it was at this moment that the beast a-borning rose to the little boy's throat, and he howled for the first time." [8] Students should read carefully the passages on Ernie's transformation to study the disturbing human reaction that overpowers Ernie. With a final blow, Ilse applauds the actions of the boys and sends Ernie into the deepest recesses of his heart.

The final paragraphs of this story illustrate the use of metaphor to create a profound image of suffering and destruction. The image of the "Rock of Woden, the Germanic god of war, storm and lords and kings"[9] represents the pagan sacrificial stone used to murder Jews in past centuries. It is a place of ultimate destruction and power and the place where Ernie must face his future. Numb and unable to feel any emotion, Ernie is obliterated from the real world. He feels no physical or emotional pain and sees his role as a "Just Man" has been destroyed. Schwarz-Bart uses language of deep proportions to define this isolation and estrangement from self. "Nothing stirred him," "obliterating," "abandoning," "emptiness," and the final declaration "I am nothing" echoes in the reader's ears.[10]

This emptiness is transformed into the most shocking of behaviors as Ernie manifests his anger and defeat into destruction and death. He becomes the perpetrator, and his victims, the insects, are the souls like him who can neither defend themselves nor rise in protest against the cruelty inflicted upon them. Schwarz-Bart uses the most beautiful symbol of freedom, the butterfly, to illustrate this, yet when Ernie kills the butterfly, he only extends his own suffering. Losing his early pledge to fulfill his legacy, he questions his righteousness: "How could he have pretended to those heights, to the even greater heights of the Just Man—he a puny rapacious insect."[11] Schwarz-Bart ends the story with the final moving statements of defeat and despair as Ernie declares to himself, "I was not a Just Man, I was nothing."[12] With power only to destroy weak victims like himself, Ernie dismembers the insects, ingests their crushed parts, and lowers himself to the position of the perpetrator of terror and violence.

This story gives students insight not just to the physical suffering of the victims of the Holocaust, but also the emotional loss as a result of their experiences. The ideas of defeat, loss of self-esteem, family legacy, choice, and human nature are all topics with which students can identify.

### Discussion Questions

The following questions can be used as a guide for the reading and discussion of the story:

▶ What historic references are made in this story to the Nazi Party's ideology?
▶ How do each of the Jewish boys represent a position Jews might take during the Holocaust?
▶ What is the difference between Ernie's and the other boys' responses to orders to sing? How does this make him a Just Man?
▶ What role does Ilse play in this story?
▶ How is Ernie's treatment of the insects a response of anger and disappointment?

---

[1] André Schwarz-Bart, "The Last of the Just," *Out of the Whirlwind: A Reader of Holocaust Literature.* Albert H. Friedlander, ed. (New York: Schocken Books, 1976), p. 85.
[2] Ibid., p. 87.
[3] Ibid.
[4] Ibid., p. 91.
[5] Ibid., p. 92.
[6] Ibid.
[7] Ibid.
[8] Ibid., p. 96.
[9] Ibid., p. 99.

## "The Quay," Ilse Aichinger

*Out of the Whirlwind: A Reader of Holocaust Literature.* Albert H. Friedlander, ed. (New York: Schocken Books), 1976. ISBN 0-8052-0925-5.

### Character List
Ellen
Bibi
Kurt
Leon
Hannah
Ruth
Herbert
George
The man who operates the swings
Two soldiers

### Plot Summary

"The Quay" is an excerpt from the novel by Aichinger titled *Herod's Children*. The title of the book is a reference to "Herod the Great" who ruled over Judaea in 74–73 BCE. During his tyrannical rule, he ordered the "Massacre of the Innocents," the killing of all male Jewish children to the age of two in an effort to destroy the rise of the prophesied "Son of God," Jesus. This biblical reference is the foundation for this story about German children living during the early days of the rise of the Nazi Party.

The story profiles a group of children who are victims of the Nuremberg Laws. Under the restrictions of the Nazis, they suffer the status of their "wrong grandparents." The main character, Ellen, emerges as a voice representing the reality of the suffering of the Jews during the Holocaust. She is a symbol of both strength and defiance.

### Objectives for Teaching "The Quay"
This story serves as an excellent tool to illustrate the power of metaphor in revealing historical fact. It is best to assign this story for one reading assignment so plot, writing style, and content can be discussed together. Teachers should focus on the following ideas:
▶ Narrative voice
▶ Lyrical quality of the writing and the use of dialogue and imagery
▶ Use of metaphor and imagery to document historical fact
▶ Imagination versus reality

### Analysis
"The Quay" opens with a group of children playing at a riverbank park, waiting for a baby to drown. The use of dialogue in the opening scene creates a marvelous

tone as Aichinger reveals the distress of these children who worry about their position in the world of Nazism. Discussing their heritage, they label each other with qualifiers based on whether or not they have "right and wrong" grandparents. This is a direct reference to the Nuremberg Laws that defined the status of Jewish citizenship by the number of Jewish grandparents one had versus "pure" German or Aryan grandparents. (See Glossary of Terms Used in Holocaust Study for further definition.) These laws forbade intermarriage of Jews and Germans, and children of these relationships were not considered true Germans. Children with "wrong grandparents" faced restrictions imposed upon them by the Nazis: they could not sit on the benches or enjoy the rides at a nearby amusement park. The children's intention is to save a German baby from drowning and redeem themselves to the mayor of the town. The drowning child represents the Christ figure and the "innocent" that Herod slaughtered who was the hope for the future of humankind.

The character Ellen becomes a measure of the other children's legitimacy. Because of her "right grandparents," she has privileges the others do not, making her an outsider in the group. The reluctance of the children to accept her as one of their own mirrors the prejudice of their surrounding society. Childhood friendship is measured by different standards in this time period, and the innocence of making a friend in childhood is forever lost.

Aichinger uses the character Ellen to develop the metaphoric qualities of storytelling. Ellen represents two voices: one of reality combined with fantasy. She is the child who simultaneously combines autobiographical detail in the fantasy of the drowned child as she weaves the plot of this rescue in an imagistic style. Her protests at saving this child are forceful. She wants no part of this scheme. In her version of the story of the drowned child, she declares, "Its mother has emigrated and its father's in the service."[1] She reveals the reality of her status as a child of mixed marriage who recognizes the impossibility of rescue. By exposing her partial illegitimacy, Ellen is accepted into the group as the other children tell of their lives. Using realistic dialogue, Aichinger develops these children through their innocent dreams and unrealistic future plans. As they catalog their wishes to be singers, football players, movie directors, and dragon-slayers, the lines between their childhood fantasies and adult terrors are exposed.

The worlds of fantasy and reality again combine in the wish to ride the carousel of swings. The swings become a metaphor of freedom and abandon.[2] The children revel in the fantasy of "And if you're lucky the chains might break" while facing the reality they may never have the opportunity to experience this. Further complicating their confusion over reality and fantasy, the character of the carousel attendant is introduced. As he gazes at the little rowboat that can hold only one, the image of "crossing over" to the other side is developed. The river becomes the passage from one side to another into death. The man has the adult voice of cynicism as he comments on the "shooting gallery" and the nature of right and wrong.[3] He articulates the voice of disillusioned adults while offering the salvation of a ride upon the swings. As the children leave Ellen to rescue the baby, they depart for a time mixed with childhood joy and terror. In a triumphant moment, they defy the law of the Nazis but also suffer the terror of the "ride." "[The children] flew against the law of their heavy shoes and against the law of the secret police. They flew according to the law of centrifugal force." [4] The ride is both the fantasy of release and the anguish of being captured.

The story takes a turn when the baby is rescued from the waters of the river. Now the river becomes the baptismal water, the waters of rebirth transforming Ellen. While the returning children are horrified at their missed opportunity for heroism, they chastise Ellen for her behavior. Again, she is the outsider, the one who has stolen their promise of the future. George, the dragonslayer, tries to comfort Ellen and leads the children to the benches in defiance of the law. It is the character of the officer that emboldens Ellen. Recognizing her father, she gains power to control the situation. "But she was not to be stopped. Her confidence lifted her like a tornado from the midst of pain and bitterness of her disappointment, and landed her in the wasteland of an unmasked country." [5] Ellen confronts her father, hugs him, and bites his cheek to leave her mark. His brutality is juxtaposed against her strength of purpose as she encourages the children to flee.

Aichinger leaves the reader with a dark and foreboding line of foreshadowing: "Like a bridge, the moon threw her shadow over to the other bank." [6] With little hope of the future for Ellen and these children, their deliverance will come only in the "crossing over to the other side."

## Discussion Questions

In teaching this story, students should record all the metaphorical images they recognize. The following questions can be used as a guide for the reading and discussion of the story:

▶ Why does Ellen appear to be the "outsider" to the other children?
▶ How is the image of shunning and torturing the outsider supported by the Nazi regime?
▶ How is this story a combination of fact and fiction, reality and fantasy?
▶ Where do we hear the cynical voice of adulthood?
▶ Define the following symbols: the carousel, the river, and the baby.
▶ Why is it not a victory at first for Ellen to have rescued the baby?
▶ Describe Ellen's father. How does he typify the German prototype of a "true" Aryan?
▶ How does the use of dialogue enhance the telling of this story?

[1] Ilse Aichinger, "The Quay," excerpt from *Herod's Children, Out of the Whirlwind: A Reader of Holocaust Literature*. Albert H. Friedlander, ed. (New York: Schocken Books 1976), p. 106.
[2] Ibid., p. 107.
[3] Ibid., p. 109.
[4] Ibid., p. 117.
[5] Ibid.
[6] Ibid., p. 118.

## "A Scrap of Time," Ida Fink

*A Scrap of Time and Other Stories*, translated from the Polish by Madeline Levine and Francine Prose (New York: Pantheon Books), 1987. ISBN 0-394-55806-5.

### Character List
> Narrator (unnamed)
> David

### Plot Summary

*A Scrap of Time*, by Ida Fink, is a collection of short stories about the Holocaust. Using the first-person voice of a young girl, Fink paints a vivid and disturbing picture of the memories of loss and suffering during and after the war. Using a lyrical and storytelling voice, Fink transforms fact into poetic language that paints a picture of the beauty and horror in this young woman's life.

### Objectives for Teaching "A Scrap of Time"

"A Scrap of Time" provides teachers with an opportunity to examine the power of fiction to recreate the facts of the Holocaust. Study of this piece will illustrate the following:
> ▶ Use of first-person narrative
> ▶ Use of metaphor and descriptive detail to combine historical fact with fiction
> ▶ Historical documentation of the roundups, deportations, and mass killings of Jews by the Nazis

### Analysis

The first story of the collection shares the title of the book. The tale combines the multiple layers of testimony and remembrance in the metaphoric context of time. Fink defines the events of the story in measurements of time, labeling the past and the present as two separate entities. The "second time" is the present "measured in months and years," and the "first time" refers to the events of the Holocaust.[1] The narrator distinguishes these two time periods purposefully, placing the brutality of her memory in its own sphere, fearing that "this second time had crushed the first and destroyed it" within her.[2] This time metaphor is developed to illustrate the duplexity of the lives of Holocaust survivors. They measure their experiences in the language of before and after and struggle with the fear of loss of memory. Fink further delineates the definition of time by the terms "action" and "roundup."[3] An "action" was a military police operation which gathered the Jews in the ghettos and towns of Eastern Europe for extermination. The term "roundup" implied a gathering of people for work in the labor battalions. Fink calls the action in her town "a scrap of time," a small moment in its history that destroyed the fabric of her childhood and the lives of all the villagers.[4]

Fink uses the collective pronoun "we" as she tells the story of her village. Speaking in *sotto voce*, the narrator portrays the victims of the action as the symbolic representation of all Jews. She defines her people in their unconscious denial of the future as those who possess a "poverty of imagination."[5] In a sympathetic but biting voice, Fink sees that the innocence of the Jews leads them to ignore the warning signs. Understanding that disobedience is not an option, the narrator views the Jews as compliant, hopeful for a peaceful future, "like infants."[6] Students should read these passages on pages 4–5 for the tone of the author. A cynical voice emerges from under the sorrowful account of memory. Fink uses this voice to speak in the collective unconscious of a people condemned to death.

The story's middle section creates the lyrical description of the countryside that acts as a temporary barrier to the atrocities in the town. On her way to the town, the main character traverses the fields brimming with summer flowers. She skips stones joyfully across the stream and then is stopped cold by the scene below her in the town square. The view from above creates an Elysian atmosphere of pastoral delights witnessing horrific incidents. The narrator observes that "time measured in the ordinary way stopped."[7] The measure of time in their lives will be forever marked by this experience, as the "second time" becomes the "first." Memory will start with the disappearance of the men and be preserved in the story of David, the narrator's cousin.

In this story, the narrative of David's fate is representative of all the Jewish victims of the Holocaust. Although David has the possibility to save himself, as one of the "Impatient Ones,"[8] he seals his fate. The tone of this labeling by the narrator challenges the motives of the Jews who surrendered themselves to the Nazis. The eyes of the narrator see a people too eager to believe the lies told to them, too committed to the solidarity of their community, and too trusting of the leaders of their town. "It was a thought that came in a flash: to be together with everyone."[9] The narrator perceives that David and thousands of other men and women marched together to their deaths.

Fink ends this story with a disturbing awakening of David and those left behind. Pleading for his mother's forgiveness, he gains "that horrifying clarity of vision that comes just before death."[10] Fink depicts the voices of men and women questioning and regretting their complicity in their deaths. The false postcards that come after the action reveal the death of the rabbi and the massacre of these blameless victims. In an ironic twist, the beauty of the countryside is transformed into the extermination site and the sanctity of the forest becomes the burying ground of the Jews. The Jews' trust in humankind is forever lost with the reality that filters from witnesses of the mass grave, and David's plea for forgiveness is shared by the people of the town who suffer the pain of surviving.

The story "A Scrap of Time" allows students to be aware of the significance of community to the Jews. Complicity of the victims of the Holocaust is a disturbing idea, one that Fink introduces in a bitter and solemn voice. For further discussion of this topic, a supplemental reading of the essay by Bruno Bettelheim titled "The Ignored Lesson of Anne Frank"[11] is informative. It raises some important questions about defiance and fate. Teachers should also consult the introduction and chapter on Primo Levi's *If Not Now, When?* (page 75) for a complete discussion of the Jewish resistance movement during the war.

### Discussion Questions

The following questions can be used as a guide for the reading and discussion of the story:

▶ How is the metaphor of measured time woven into the telling of the story? What does it represent?

▶ In several places in the story, the narrator speaks of "we." Why is this a significant use of the pronoun?

▶ What fateful decision does David make? How does he represent millions of Jews during the Holocaust?

▶ How is nature and beauty juxtaposed against the images of death in this story?

▶ Why is the narrator of the story never named?

[1] Ida Fink, *A Scrap of Time and Other Stories.* Translated from the Polish by Madeline Levine and Francine Prose (New York: Pantheon Books, 1987), p. 3.

[2] Ibid.

[3] Ibid., p. 4.

[4] Ibid.

[5] Ibid., p. 5.

[6] Ibid.

[7] Ibid., p. 6.

[8] Ibid., p. 7.

[9] Ibid., p. 8.

[10] Ibid., p. 9.

[11] Bruno Bettelheim, "The Ignored Lesson of Anne Frank," *Surviving and Other Essays* (New York: Vintage Books, 1952), pp. 246–57.

# Stones from the River

Ursula Hegi (New York: Scribner Paperback Fiction), 1994. ISBN 0-671-78-75-1.

## Character List

Gertrude Montag
Leo Montag
Trudi Montag
Emil Hespring
Herr and Frau Abramowitz
Ilse Abramowitz
Frau Weiler
Georg Weiler
Frau Rosen
Eva Rosen
Renate Eberhardt
Helmut Eberhardt
Max Rudnick

Because this novel is extensive in its use of characters to reveal the story, students should keep a character journal. This journal should have the name of each character on a page and the student should note the important actions and characteristics of the individual throughout the novel.

## Plot Summary

> And what [Trudi] wanted more than anything . . . was for all the differences between people to matter no more—difference in size and race and belief—differences that had become a justification for destruction.[1]

*Stones from the River* is a rich and complicated novel about life in a small German town between the years of 1915 and 1952. The events of the story are seen through the eyes of young Trudi Montag, a dwarf, or *Zwerg* in German. Hegi creates the analogy between the "otherness" of Trudi and the persecution of the Jews during World War II. As Trudi struggles to define her place in the community amidst the rising world of Nazism, the reader is introduced to a panoply of characters who give vivid detail to the passion, discrimination, violence, and silence of this small town. With detailed metaphor, strong descriptive passages, and careful examination of characters, Hegi provides the reader a study of Germany from the early days of the war to the aftermath of the Holocaust. The novel weaves into the story clear historical reference, creating a model of the experiences of the German and Jewish communities during the war.

The author's writing style allows reading on many different levels. The narrative story is engaging and involves the reader with the easy flow of story-telling and character development. Teaching this novel provides a prime opportunity for students of all levels to focus on how a writer develops the events of the story through meticulous characterization. The writing and presentation activities for the book include the study of character analysis. The novel also provides a historical reference in narrative voice of the significant events of the war. Teachers should consult the Glossary of Terms Used in Holocaust Study to help in creating a rich vocabulary for Holocaust study.

### Objectives for Teaching *Stones from the River*

This novel gives students an opportunity to gain insight into the prejudices that existed in a small town in Germany before and during World War II. Teachers should consider the following ideas in their analysis of the novel:

▶ To examine the social and political life in a small German town
▶ To reference the historical events of World War II and the Holocaust
▶ To study the use of character development
▶ To study the analogy of Trudi Montag and the war through the representative metaphors of the novel

### Part One: Creating a German Town

Patience and obedience—they were inseparable. . . .[2]

The early chapters of this novel are designed to create a picture of life in Burgdorf, Germany. Several major themes emerge, helping to define the moral structure and belief system of the German people during this time in history. The town emerges as an encapsulated community where there are clear distinctions between class and religious belief. Through her narrative voice, Hegi provides an examination of the specific elements that control the town.

### The Role of the Catholic Church

Hegi uses the introductory chapters of this novel to reveal the significant role of the Catholic Church in this community. The Church emerges as a patriarchal figure that establishes the moral and social codes for the town. With analytical emphasis on the Church's demand for attendance and obedience to the strict laws that govern the Church, Hegi allows the reader to examine the complex development of the German psyche. Students should look carefully for the characteristics of the Church that mold its members' lives. With strong reference to the power and authority of God, the reader sees the people of Burgdorf as devout and strictly trained. Children learn at a young age that "Acts of disobedience were punished efficiently: a slap on your knuckles with a ruler; three rosaries; confinement."[3] Children are taught respect for parents, teachers, and government, and their beliefs are supported by regular attendance at mass and religious school. The Church provides education, and all aspects of life are examined and regulated by the priests and nuns.

Careful consideration should be given to the traditions that the Church establishes for the people. Discussion should focus on the role of the religious icon of the Church and the physical as well as spiritual traditions that govern its members. Discussion should examine the following ideas as revealed in the narrative of the story:

▶ The role of the daily mass
▶ The importance of the choir to the community and Trudi
▶ The power of the setting of the Catholic Church: the ritual of incense, prayer, communion

The Church influences Trudi as a child. She dedicates herself to prayer for her body to grow. The passion of her devotion causes her to believe in a God who can change her from the *Zwerg* of the town to a normal young girl. To Trudi, the Church becomes the vehicle for disappointment. God responds to her prayers with a "twisted horrible joke"[4] that does not elongate her limbs, but only widens her torso.

The definition of sin unveils much about the values of the town. Careful examination of sin can be found on pages 86–87 where the reader is given a litany of the evils of the world as defined in Burgdorf, Germany. These passages also give insight to the character Leo Montag as he establishes the moral code that governs his family: "There are things . . . that the Church calls sins, but they are part of being human. And those we need to embrace. The most important thing . . . is to be kind."[5] He represents the voice of reason and compassion versus religious zeal and admonishment.

The Church also provides the vocabulary of intolerance and religious exclusivity that becomes the foundation of the Nazi Party. Children are taught at a young age to recognize pagan babies, the power of Lucifer, the fear of Purgatory, and the all-encompassing awareness of sin. It is important for students to carefully trace the anti-Semitism that reigns in this town. Journal work could catalog the incidents and definitions of discrimination, focusing on what "facts" about the Jews are taught to children (pp. 105–06). For example:

▶ The views of the Protestant church
▶ Jews as killers of Jesus
▶ Jews as drinkers of Christian blood

Hegi uses the role of the Church to illustrate the paradox of the rising tide of hatred that envelops the Germans. As they burn the homes of their Jewish neighbors and deliver to the Nazis their fellow members of the community, the congregants remain devout and pious. Their actions are never judged as sin. As Trudi struggles with the violence and power within her to hurt other people, she recognizes that the people of Burgdorf use prayer to silence their guilt. "Once they got beyond the kneeling in the somber confessional, [the townspeople] looked forward to the Saturday absolutions that turned their souls white and glowing."[6] Trudi acts as a model of human behavior for the power to change. She learns to reject cruelty and sees the good she can accomplish in her life through action.

The study of the role of the Catholic Church in Germany and the precedent of anti-Semitism in Eastern Europe is a rich research topic for students. Teachers should refer to the Suggested Reading for articles and books that examine these two aspects of German history.

### Writing and Presentation Ideas

1. Anti-Semitism has a long history in European culture. Divide the class into small groups and assign a section of Europe. Students should research the roots of anti-Semitism in their region, noting any significant political and social action taken against Jews. A large map can be drawn and labeled for a class project, with an oral sharing of ideas. (See Suggested Reading for research sources.)

2. Hegi provides a meticulous setting for her novel, complete with physical detail of the placement of houses, the Catholic Church, businesses, and the river. Students could illustrate a map of the town of Burgdorf labeling important sites.

3. Trudi expresses so much of the novel's emotion. Choosing several moving and significant events in Trudi's life, students could create a diary for Trudi in her voice. Writing should include the detail of the story combined with the student's imagination of expression. A physical diary should be presented as the final project.

4. Students interested in video could make a film of their hometown. Visual imagery could include a tour of the town with its significant architectural and geographical sites. The video could include interviews of important community members relating memories of the town's history. This could be completed as a group project for the class dividing the students into groups: video crew, interview group, and the writers of the narrator's voice-over.

## Part Two: Development of Character as Analogy to War

*Stones from the River*, an important document about human nature, is significant because it gives the reader unusual insight into the German personality during the war. Hegi helps the reader to understand the philosophical and sociological elements that controlled the behavior of the people in this time period. Through her meticulous characterization, we see the violence, repression, discrimination, love, and compassion of the people of Burgdorf.

### The Women of Burgdorf

The early events of this novel catalog the role of women in the years during and after World War I. Students should read about the conditions of German life during World War I, noting the poverty and despair of the people. (See Suggested Reading for research ideas.) Because the male population was absent, women in the community of Burgdorf gained status as more than the caretakers of their homes. Hegi writes: "It was the summer of 1915, and the town belonged to women."[7] Although spinsterhood and single parents were traditionally scorned in this town, students should examine carefully the power women possessed during this time (pp. 12–13). Traditional German values kept women in the background, but this is a Germany that sees women running the town and businesses as they raise their children. Discussion can focus on the difference between Burgdorf before the men return from war and after.

## Gertrude Montag

The story of Trudi Montag begins with the marvelous description of her mother Gertrude. Gertrude emerges in the early stages of this novel as a woman profoundly disturbed. "[They] sensed that seed of craziness in Gertrude long before it flourished."[8] With unique reference to the power of the Church, Gertrude Montag emerges as a passionately devout Christian who is tortured by her sense of self. "[The priest] forgave her the one sin she could never forgive herself."[9] Students should focus on the following ideas in their study of Gertrude and her relationship to her daughter:

- ▶Gertrude's behavior after the birth of Trudi (p. 13)
- ▶The role of the Church and its definition of sin for Gertrude (p. 14)
- ▶The relationship with Emil Hespring (p. 30)
- ▶The stones in Gertrude's knee (p. 30)
- ▶The significance of hiding under the porch (p. 14)
- ▶Gertrude's "imprisonment" in her home and Teresienheim (p. 23)
- ▶Gertrude's obsession with giving birth again (pp. 34–37)
- ▶Gertrude's death (pp. 41–42)

Gertrude's character sets the foundation for the development of Trudi. Trudi becomes the symbol of shame by the events of her birth and her dwarfism. She is the punishment for Gertrude's indiscretion and the physical embodiment of sin. In an analogy to the fate of the Jews, Gertrude and Trudi become the "outsiders." Gertrude is excluded from a normal life because of her perceived sin, and Trudi represents the tenets of the discrimination of the Nazis: she is deformed, not normal by the party's standards, and suspect in her own town. The porch becomes the symbol of hiding and enclosure, much like the cellar that Leo and Trudi dig to protect the Jews. Under that porch, Gertrude and Trudi are united for the first time in the love between a mother and daughter; they are isolated, protected, and together. This is where Trudi and her mother establish the bond between them as "outsiders."

Further examination of the character Trudi can be found in the section titled The Power of Storytelling.

## Frau Weiler and Her Son Georg

Georg is the child of Frau Weiler, a protective and suffocating mother who refuses to allow her child to grow up. She dresses him in girl's clothes, refuses to cut his hair, and reigns over his every move. In Georg, Trudi finds a companion with whom she can identify her "otherness," and Georg Weiler becomes the childhood friend who joins her in a shared state of isolation. "She accepted his difference so much

Books

easier than her own. . . ."[10] The death of his father in the confusing accident/suicide provides the foundation for their sharing. His "otherness" becomes her refuge, and although Trudi wants Georg to be happy, she is terrified of his transformation into one of "them." Georg is a figure whose very differences make him susceptible to the enticing lies of the Nazi Party. Later in the novel, the Nazi Party will provide the community in which Georg has spent his life striving to belong. Students should focus on the early relationship between Trudi and Georg, and the culminating violence and cruelty he bestows upon her. Research into the Nazi Youth Movement will give insight to the character and the analogies to the war.

### Leo Montag

Hegi provides a unique character in her development of Leo, Trudi's father. Returning from war as a wounded hero, Leo reigns over the pay library with his gentle tone and compassionate ear for listening. Leo represents the best of human nature. He nurtures his daughter, supports his friends, and acts as a moral compass for the town. Students should make careful note of Leo's behavior as an oppositional view to the events of World War II. Specific areas to examine:

> ▶Leo's relationship with Gertrude and Trudi
> ▶His role as the town librarian
> ▶His relationship with other members of the community: Frau Weiler, Frau Rosen, Emil Hespring, and the Abramowitz family
> ▶Leo's relationship with the Catholic Church
> ▶His role as one of the "Righteous Few"

### The Abramowitz Family

The creation of this family allows Hegi to profile an assimilated Jewish family in Germany during the war. Herr Abramowitz is a wealthy lawyer who fought bravely for his country in World War I. A member of the upper class of Burgdorf, he is respected for his education and refinement, but his status is also a point of resentment for the community. Students should read carefully for the rising hatred that overtakes the town toward this family. Questions they might consider:

> ▶What sets this family apart from the community?
> ▶How do Herr Abramowitz's politics and position isolate him in this community?
> ▶How does this family's sense of nationalism prevent their escape from the Nazis?
> (See Part Three for further discussion ideas.)

There are a number of secondary characters who add depth to this story. Students should take notes on the development of Frau Doctor Rosen and her family, Klaus Malter, the Man Who Touches His Heart, the Secret Benefactor, Max Rudnick, and Frau Eberhardt and her son Helmut.

### Writing and Presentation Ideas

1. Characterization is an important writing style in this novel. Students could write a character study of a family member or friend in a narrative voice. They should reveal the significant personality traits and behavior of their subject through action and dialogue.

2. The "Righteous Few" is a term used for the people of Europe who aided Jews in their flight from the Nazis. Several books have been written about these brave individuals. Students should research one of these people for a class presentation. They should consider the following ideas:

▶ Where did the person live?

▶ What was the person's role in the community before the war?

▶ What did this person do to protect Jews from the Nazis?

(See Suggested Reading for research sources.)

3. Students should create a "lending library" for their classmates. Focusing on the events of the Holocaust, students should research a bibliography of fiction and personal narrative of the Holocaust. Each student should design and create a book jacket for their book choice. The jacket should include an inner flap with plot summary and biographical notes on the author. Projects could be displayed in the library for other students to view. School librarians are a tremendous support for the research of this project.

## Part Three: The Power of Storytelling

> And it was not even that she made up anything, but rather that she listened closely to herself.[11]

The power of storytelling has significance in this novel. With a powerful narrative voice, Hegi weaves an intricate design of the character as a storyteller. We receive the images and ideas of this novel through the telescope of Trudi's eyes, and what emerges is a young girl coming of age with the support and power of storytelling.

The isolation the town imposes upon Trudi enforces the "rules" that she must stay quiet and bring little attention to herself. In her silence, Trudi spends her early childhood years attempting to stretch herself physically to fit into the community. Students should pay close attention to the silence that envelops Trudi and the community support of this loss of voice. A focus on the following ideas will help mold the early understanding of Trudi's absence of voice.

▶ The role of the nuns in the imposed silence

▶ The children's cruelty toward Trudi

▶ The story of St. Giles (p. 98)

As her otherness isolates Trudi from the community, she discovers another power within her—storytelling. Seated behind the counter of the pay library, she becomes privy to the secrets and desires of the town's people. "Her stories grew and changed as she tested them to see how far they gave . . . but all of them started from a core of what she knew and sensed about people."[12] She keeps their secrets, embellishes the details, and spreads the potency of these stories throughout the town. While carefully hiding her own secrets, Trudi uses this power in often cruel and hurtful ways. Hegi intentionally makes Trudi an imperfect human being, one that has flaws she must recognize and change. We see her rage as well as her compassion and capacity to do good. Students should focus on the following pages to gain an understanding of Trudi's storytelling: pp. 152–56 and 159.

Slowly, Trudi begins to gain strength as she recognizes her true self. Students should analyze carefully the transformation of Trudi that comes from her relationships with other characters. The dog Seehund provides an unconditional friendship that is a model for what true love is. Trudi's encounter with the other Zwerg Pia allows her to "understand that for Pia, being a Zwerg was normal and beautiful."[14] This visit awakens Trudi's sexuality and gives her permission to walk, talk, and dress as a woman.

### The Use of Metaphor

Hegi carefully weaves the analogies of war to human nature into several significant images. In their reading journals, students should take notes on the significance of stones as a representative image. Stones are the sign of shame for Gertrude, a religious icon for Trudi as a marker for her hurt and pain, and an image for love and growth with Max. The river joins the images of stones in its representative ideas. The river acts as a baptismal pool for Trudi. It is in the river that she is allowed to shed the burden of her physical self, swim, and be free. With its flooding and the deaths that occur, the river purges the town of all recognizable boundaries and rules of behavior. Its natural power rivals the violence of the German people of Burgdorf. The river is also a crossing-over point for Trudi. The act of molestation by the boys Georg, Hans-Jurgen, and Paul forces Trudi to face a turning point by that river. Students should read carefully pages 145–51 to discover the imagery of the river before and after the molestation.

### Writing and Presentation Ideas

1. German culture has a long history of storytelling through fables and fantasy. Students could research and read *Grimm's Fairytales* and other selections from German literature to discover this tradition. Reading these tales aloud to the class, students could discuss the connection between the fascination with dwarfs and little people and its relationship to the novel.
2. In a creative writing project, students could write their own myths and fairytales. They should consider the reader's age level and the archetypal use of mythological symbols.

## Part Four: The Rise of Nazi Power in Burgdorf

"Who shall pay for this?"[15]

Hegi uses the second section of the book to catalog the events of the Nazis' rise to power. Having established the characters and their roles in the community, Hegi then makes the experiences of their lives parallel the historical events of the Holocaust. Using a narrative voice, Hegi gives the reader a clear description of the Nazis' violent and cruel treatment of the Jews of Germany. Each character emerges as either a victim of the Nazi reign, a voice of protest, or one of silent collusion. The following are a series of events from the novel that directly parallel historical events of the war. Students should be responsible for knowing the definition of these events and ideas. Teachers can find further definitions in the Glossary of Terms Used in Holocaust Study.

▶ The *Judenboykott* (p. 164)

▶ *Fackelparade:* Torch Parade (p. 165)

▶ Hitler Jugend: Hitler Youth Movement (pp. 166, 227)

▶ 1933 book burning (p. 171)

▶ Propaganda (p. 195)

▶ Role of the Catholic Church (p. 304)

▶ *Verdammte Juden* (p. 196)

▶ *Kristallnacht* (pp. 262–63)

▶ 1938 Anschluss of Austria and Czechoslovakia (p. 280)

▶ *Konzentrationslager*: Concentration Camps (p. 258)

▶ *Kinderlandverschickung*: Evacuation of German children (p. 289)

▶ Establishing the Jewish ghetto (p. 293)

The Nuremberg Laws of 1935 were a series of laws passed by the German government defining the status of the Jews in Germany. These laws restricted the civil rights of the Jews. Students should read carefully the events surrounding the fate of the Abramowitz and Rosen families as well as other Jews in Burgdorf. The following questions can be discussed in relationship to these laws.

1. Which of these restrictions placed upon Jews are illustrated in the development of the story?

    ▶ Reich Citizenship Law: only citizens of "pure" German blood were considered citizens of Germany

    ▶ Law for the protection of German blood: the restriction of intermarriage between Germans and Jews

    ▶ Prevention of employment of Germans in Jewish households and businesses

    ▶ The confiscation of all Jewish private property by the Nazi Party

    ▶ Confiscation of all Jewish passports to be stamped "J" for identification

    ▶ Wearing of the yellow star

    ▶ The prohibition of owning radios, bicycles, telephones

    ▶ Prohibition of attendance at public schools

    ▶ Establishment of the ghettos (p. 293)

Students should take notes on the references to these laws and the effect they have on the relationship between Eva, Ilse, and their husbands. Careful attention to Frau Simon's arrest will provide further discussion of the Nazi regime. Which characters are supporters of the Nazis and who protests their takeover?

## Writing and Presentation Ideas

1. The enactment of the Nuremberg Laws was an essential tool for the Nazi Party. Students should research these laws, looking for primary documents that give evidence to their existence.

2. The Nazi Youth Movement helped define the power of the Reich upon the young people of Germany. Students should research the role of this organization and how it strengthened the party. Students can also look for examples of

the propaganda disseminated promoting the Youth Movement with posters and billboards. A class presentation of the propaganda of the Third Reich could include video footage and photography. (See Videography for film ideas.)

3. Students should investigate the definition Hitler imposed for a perfect Aryan nation. How does the theory of Social Darwinism become the foundation for Hitler's atrocities against the victims of the Holocaust?

4. The Wannsee Conference was where the Germans first used the phrase "The Final Solution." Students should find primary documents from this conference and discuss the language use and specific details of this plan. (See Suggested Reading.)

## Part Five: Action versus Silence and Collusion

"Fear . . . is a strange thing. It strips off masks. . . . In some people it brings out the lowest instincts, while others become more compassionate. Both have to do with survival. But the choice is ours." [16]

In the final section of this book, Hegi reveals the moral dilemma the people of Germany had to face during the war. They have the choice to help the Jews of their town or escape behind closed doors in silence. Hegi uses this idea of choice to illustrate the growth Trudi experiences while aiding the Jews who are trying to escape the Nazis. "Working with the others on the tunnel—dirty, sweating, and aching—she felt more of a sense of belonging to a community than she ever had before." [17] Students should consider the following events in discussing Trudi's strength and purpose:

▶ The hiding of the young mother and child
▶ Digging the tunnel
▶ Trudi's arrest
▶ Her relationship with Max Rudnick

At the end of the book, Hegi gives a frank and interesting discussion of the sentiment and events after Germany's defeat. The townspeople are burdened by the secrets they share about the past events in their town, and they remain resentful and angry with the Jewish people for their defeat. Hegi expands the silence that engulfs the people as the returning soldiers refuse to share their experiences and participation in the atrocities of the war. "Despite the façade of togetherness, Trudi would notice the fracture between families, the numbing that many found with alcohol, the shame in the eyes of some wives when they walked at the arms of their husbands." [18] Reading carefully pages 449–73, students should focus on the following questions:

▶ How does the role of women change as their husbands return from the war?
▶ What is the sentiment toward the Jews and the Americans after the war?
▶ To what do the Germans attribute their losses?
▶ What is the town's response to the truth of the camps and the atrocities performed there?
▶ What reaction do the Germans have to the war crimes and trials after the war?
▶ What are the living conditions in Burgdorf after the war?
▶ What are the Germans' feelings about Hitler?

►How does Burgdorf define "back to normal"?

At the conclusion of the novel, Trudi comes full circle in her understanding of self and her place in the community. "Working with Emil Hespring and the fugitives had taught her what it was like to belong, that you could initiate it, build it, be it." [19] Suffering the loss of Max and her father, she reflects on that yearning she felt to be a part of the community, to be normal. Her participation in the rescue of Jews allows her to see her purpose in life, to recognize that her true self is within, not defined by the physical appearance of her body. Trudi realizes it is the strength from inside herself that allows her to triumph over the evils of the world.

## Writing and Presentation Ideas

1. The monument to Hitler is destroyed at the end of the novel. Students could design a fitting monument for the victims of the Holocaust. Students could work in teams researching the present monuments around the world and create a three-dimensional model of their monument. Presentations to the class and display by the school would be recommended. (See Art chapter.)

2. Students could conduct interviews of veterans of World War II. Of particular interest would be liberators of the camps. Students could work in pairs to determine the questions they might ask. Teachers should consult with local libraries for a "speaker list" or the local organization for Veterans of Foreign Wars. Interviews could be videotaped or written and presented to the class.

3. Many books have been written about the ghetto protests and uprisings against the Germans. Students should be divided into small groups to research the ghettos of Warsaw, Vilna, and Lodz. Film footage is available for supplemental lessons as well as personal narrative on tape and the Internet. (See Suggested Reading for research ideas.)

## Suggested Reading

Dawidowicz, Lucy. *The War Against the Jews: 1933–1945.* 10th ed. New York: Bantam Books, 1986.

Hilberg, Raul. *The Destruction of the European Jews.* 3 vols. Rev. ed. New York: Holmes and Meir, 1985.

*The Holocaust,* Yad Vashem: Publications and Research.

Innocenti, Robert. *Rose Blanche.* Translated by Martha Coventry and Richard Graglia. Mankato, Minnesota: Creative Education, 1985.

Isaacman, Clara. *Clara's Story.* Philadelphia: Jewish Publication Society of America, 1984.

Katz, Jacob. *From Prejudice to Anti-Semitism.* Cambridge: Harvard University Press, 1980.

*Lvov Ghetto Diary*. Translated by Jerzy Michalowicz. Amherst: University of Massachusetts Press, 1990.

Scholl, Inge. *Students Against Tyranny: The Resistance of the White Rose, Munich*, 1942–1943. Middletown, CT: Wesleyan University Press, 1983.

Zuckerman, Yitzchak ("Antek"). *A Surplus of Memory: Chronicle of the Warsaw Ghetto Uprising*. Translated by Barbara Harshaw. Berkeley, Los Angeles, Oxford: University of California Press, 1993.

**Videography**

*Dietrich Bonhoeffer: Memories and Perspectives*. First Run, Icarus Films.

*Not in Our Town: Heroes*, 1993. Social Studies School Services.

*The Triumph of the Will*, Leni Riefenstahl, 1934. Social Studies School Services.

*The Warsaw Ghetto*, Great Britain, 1968. Social Studies School Services.

*The White Rose*, West Germany, 1982. Social Studies School Services.

**Books**

---

[1] Ursula Hegi, *Stones from the River* (New York: Scribner Paperback Fiction, 1994). p. 336.

[2] Ibid., p. 10.

[3] Ibid.

[4] Ibid.

[5] Ibid., p. 86.

[6] Ibid., p. 122.

[7] Ibid., p. 11.

[8] Ibid., p. 13.

[9] Ibid., p. 14.

[10] Ibid., p. 80.

[11] Ibid., p. 101.

[12] Ibid.

[13] Ibid., p. 123.

[14] Ibid., p. 134.

[15] Ibid., p. 270.

[16] Ibid., p. 310.

[17] Ibid., p. 331.

[18] Ibid., p. 449.

[19] Ibid., p. 521.

# Seed of Sarah

Memoirs of a Survivor, Judith Magyar Isaacson (Chicago and Urbana: University of Illinois Press), 1991. ISBN 0-252-06219-1

## Glossary

**Anti-Semitism.** Hostility toward Jews

**Aryanization.** "Aryan" was originally the language spoken by Indo-European people. The Nazis used the term to characterize the "race" of Germans "superior" to all other races

**Concentration Camp.** Prisons for political prisoners, religious dissidents, and "non-Aryan" people; by the end of World War II, the Germans had established more than one hundred major camps

**Deportation.** Forced transport to a place of incarceration

**Ghetto.** See Glossary of Terms Used in Holocaust Study

**Jewish Laws of the Hungarian Government.** A series of laws passed by the government imposing restrictions on Jews

**Kapo.** From the Latin "capo" meaning "head"; a term used in the concentration camps and death camps to designate inmates who worked as functionaries of the camp; the kapos oversaw work detail and daily rituals of their fellow inmates and received privileges for their compliance with the Nazis

**Labor Battalions.** Work forces comprised of prisoners used as slave laborers

**Nationalism.** Devotion to one's own nation

**Pogrom.** Organized acts of violence against the Jews of Eastern Europe

**Prejudice.** An opinion formed before the facts are known, based on rumors, myth, ignorance, lies, and fear

**Seed of Sarah.** Biblical reference to the future generations of Abraham and Sarah; the Jews

**Shtetl.** A small Jewish town or village

**Star of David.** The yellow star all Jews were forced to wear; the badge used by the Nazis for identification in the occupied countries during World War II; a six-cornered yellow star with the word "Jude" or "Jew" written across it

**Transit.** Label for the train bound for the concentration camps with deported prisoners

**Yom Kippur.** Jewish High Holy Day of Atonement

**Zähl Appell.** Systematic lineup and counting of concentration camp inmates

### Character List

> Judith Magyar Isaacson
> Rózsa (Judith's mother)
> Jani Klein (Judith's father)
> The Uncles Laci, Feri, Józsi
> Aunt Magda
> Sidonia and Simon Klein (paternal grandparents)
> Józsa and Lajos Vágó (maternal grandparents)
> Dr. Fredrich Biczó
> Ilona Pogány
> Irving Isaacson

### Plot Summary

The event ended my childhood.[1]

The personal testimony of Judith Magyar Isaacson starts in the town of Kaposvar, Hungary, and takes the reader through the horrifying events of life in the concentration camp Auschwitz-Birkenau. Through her clear and articulate voice, Isaacson details her life, from the forced labor units to her miraculous liberation and immigration to the United States.

The predominant themes Isaacson weaves through her narrative are the historical significance of the events, the solidarity of family, the principles of human behavior, both good and evil, and the perseverance of the human spirit to capture a dream. Teaching this narrative gives teachers an opportunity to examine personal writing as a literary style that combines universal themes and historical events as its foundation.

Close analysis of the text allows a careful study of writing style and encourages several writing prompts in the genre of personal narrative.

### Objectives for *Teaching Seed of Sarah*

*Seed of Sarah* is a book rich in both its historical information and its voice of personal memoir. In considering the following objectives, teachers should examine both the significance of the narrative voice and the historical reference.

▶To understand the historical significance of the events of Isaacson's testimony

▶To examine principles of humanity: Good and Evil

▶To understand fantasy and reality: dreams, deportation, liberation, immigration, and return

▶To use the writing genre of personal narrative

▶To learn research and presentation methods

## Part One: A Historical Perspective

The beginning of *Seed of Sarah* gives historical information about the early events of the Holocaust. Through the detailed and accurate voice of Isaacson as a young girl growing up in Hungary, students are able to build a vocabulary and foundation for the factual information.

The story opens in the spring of 1938. Germany has just annexed Austria and taken parts of Czechoslovakia. The "Aryanization" of Jewish businesses and property in Germany has begun, and Hitler is defining his systematic extermination of the "Inferior Race." Through her narrative, Judith depicts the life of a normal, healthy teenager. The opening chapters of the book give details of a Jewish family who has assimilated into the community of Kaposvar. Her family is portrayed as a tightly knit group with both sets of grandparents alive and numerous uncles and aunts who color Judith's daily routine. Well-educated, private-business owners and workers, Judith's parents are strong nationalists, as proven by her father and uncles who fought against Germany as officers in the Hungarian army during World War I.

The portrait of Judith as a schoolgirl illustrates the assimilation of some Jews in the Eastern European communities. Judith studies in a school of mixed religions, and her academic world shows a strong affiliation with the Hungarian nationalism her family embraced. She is a young woman who relishes the beauty of the Hungarian and German languages as she devotes herself to the study of the great European poets. Memorizing poems by the romantic poet Goethe, Judith revels in poetry and hopes to study literature at the Sorbonne. Her romantic ideals, embodied in the pastoral language of Goethe, are lost in the deportation to the camps. Teachers should read with students several poems by Goethe to establish the early passions and dreams of Isaacson.

Judith's experiences in school parallel the anti-Semitic strains of Eastern Europe as Germany begins to take over. Preparing for her recitation of a nationalist poem on the March 15th celebration of the Hungarian Revolution, Judith is frightened by the BBC announcement that the "Jewish women are on their hands and knees mopping up Vienna's promenade."[2] This terrifying invasion of Austria begins the changes for the Jews in Eastern Europe, including Judith and her family. When Judith delivers the recitation of the poem, she is insulted by the audience who shout at her, "Shut up, Jewess,"[3] and her childhood comes to an abrupt end. In 1941 Hungary declares war on the Soviet Union and the rumors of concentration camps and the rape of young girls sent to the Russian front plague Judith and her family. In the summer of 1944, as the Americans are landing on the beaches of Normandy, Judith and her family are transported to the death camp Auschwitz-Birkenau.

The approaching reign of terror by the Germans is detailed by the narrative account of events in this family's life. Students should focus on the following significant ideas and events of the story:

> ▶ Discrimination sanctions: the passing of the Jewish Laws
> ▶ Rewriting of the history books
> ▶ Deaths of the grandfathers: comparisons of the infiltration of anti-Semitism
> ▶ Name changing on legal documents
> ▶ Immigration laws
> ▶ Numerus Clausus
> ▶ Jewish Labor Units
> ▶ Deterioration of living conditions
> ▶ Occupation of homes and businesses by Germans
> ▶ Mandate of the wearing of the Star of David
> ▶ Ghettoization of the Jews
> ▶ Deterioration of quality of life: food, shelter, and employment

Students should be responsible for the definition of these events and note in their response journals references to the specific events through textual examination. Teachers can use these ideas to develop class discussions and group presentations. (See Introduction: Teaching Tools.)

## Presentation Ideas

The reading of *Seed of Sarah* provides teachers with several group presentation ideas focusing on historical events. Students should be divided into small groups and be provided with detailed outlines for research methods and presentation expectations. The following are two suggestions for projects that will give solid historical and social background for the reading of the text.

1. Divide the class into two groups. One group of students should be responsible for creating a timeline for Judith Isaacson's journey. The other group should create a parallel historical line that details the events of Hitler's regime. Students from group one should focus on textual proof for their research, including the significant historical and personal events. Students in group two will need to do research on the historical events. The groups will work together to format methods of presentation. This is a good opportunity for students to use graphing and visual aids from a computer program (where available). Encourage students to include documentation and visual aids on their timeline to develop the facts more fully.

2. Students could prepare a class presentation on the history of events leading up to World War II. Groups of students could be divided in their research in the following ways:

▶World War I and the impact of the Treaty of Versailles

▶History of the Weimar Republic

▶Economic and social conditions of Germany from WW I to the start of WW II.

▶History of anti-Semitism in Eastern Europe

## Writing Ideas

The study of *Seed of Sarah* is developmentally appropriate for high-school students in terms of writing expectations. The connections between Judith's experiences and feelings can be made through a focus on personal essay writing. Students are constantly asking the question, "Who am I?" Personal essay writing is a place where they can begin to define their thoughts and place in the world.

Teachers should stress the basic principles of personal essay writing: writing in the first person, using narrative detail and personal anecdote, developing ideas that can be shared with a large audience, and articulating voice and style.

The following writing prompts can be used as twenty-minute in-class writings as prefaces to class discussion of the text, or as lengthier assignments which use the drafting process to refine ideas.

1. As a prewriting exercise, have students write a five-minute autobiography detailing a significant event in their lives. The five-minute prewriting gives students an opportunity to make a list of the details of the moment they will describe in a longer writing. This prewriting can develop into a lengthier autobiography project. The following suggestions can be adapted to individual classes:

   a. A written autobiography: Students should write an eight- to ten-page autobiography in personal essay form, using the narrative voice. Assignments should be over several weeks, with a series of two- to three-page essays due each week. These essays will be the foundation for their finished product. Encourage students to include the following details:

      ▶Heritage and family history

      ▶Definition of family relationships

      ▶Religion

      ▶Education

      ▶Patriotism

      ▶Personal experiences of significance that define their ideas, beliefs, and future expectations

   Teachers should encourage narrative voice to "tell a story" of important events in their lives in an anecdotal style.

   b. An autobiographical poster: Students should make a poster of their lives. The poster could include photographs, childhood mementos, poetry, magazine collage, and drawings by the student. Their posters should tell the story of their lives with vivid, visual detail.

Books

## Part Two: The Principles of Humanity: Good and Evil

"It is better to suffer an injustice than to commit one."[4]

The study of Holocaust literature provides a rich and important means for students to discover and discuss the difficult issues raised in the lives of the inmates in the concentration camps. The second area of study for *Seed of Sarah* is a focus on the moral and ethical issues of survival in an unrelenting amoral situation. The idea of moral and ethical choices is predominant in this testimony. Objectives for the study of internment in Auschwitz-Birkenau should focus discussion on the following themes about choice:

> ▶ Good and evil human behavior
> ▶ Independence and imprisonment
> ▶ Individuality and anonymity
> ▶ Myths and realities
> ▶ Courage and cowardice
> ▶ Truth and lying
> ▶ Dreams and reality

As Judith, her mother, aunt, and two grandmothers board the cattle car for Auschwitz-Birkenau, the words of her grandfather echo in her ears. "Listen! Don't be afraid to speak to any man. Soldiers may be beasts on the battlefield, but they all had a mother, just like you and me."[5] This credo begins a discussion on the ethics of human behavior. Grandfather Klein's remarks reflect the important realization for students that individuality does exist, even in a concentration camp. To look a human being in the eye and give testimony to his or her humanity is a step in denying the anonymity of life in a camp. As Judith is confronted with atrocities of behavior in Auschwitz-Birkenau, she begins to gain insight into what one must do to survive. There are several events in this section of the testimony that should be carefully analyzed in terms of the predominant themes listed above. The following ideas are suggestions for daily discussion topics and writing activities:

> ▶ Detail of the "routine of a transport": deportation regime, cattle cars
> ▶ The rituals of arrival at Auschwitz-Birkenau: selection, showers, shaving, tattooing, clothes, barracks, work detail, *Zähl Appell*
> ▶ Landscape and physical setting
> ▶ Lack of privacy and modesty

Students should record these moments (and others) of both good and evil behavior, noting pages from the text and their reactions to the events of the story.

Choice becomes a resounding theme in this section of the book. Faced with several terrifying camp selections and threats to family solidarity and survival, Judith is plagued at all times with decisions of unparalleled import. Judith makes choices about her role as a Kapo, stealing and bartering, and work-detail relationships with her fellow inmates. Throughout the telling of her tale, Isaacson stresses the decisions that are moral and inherently good despite the prevalence of violence and evil around her. Students should keep a journal of specific choices Isaacson and her family make in order to survive. Which choices define or challenge the foundation of their beliefs? How do the words of Grandfather Klein act as a guide in their choice making?

Isaacson also portrays the moral and traditional values to which the Jews cling in their desperate attempts to maintain their dignity as both human beings and Jews. Through her descriptive accounts of the celebration of the Jewish high holidays, the joining of voices in prayer and song, the sharing of a crust of bread, and the constant affirmation of the importance of family, Isaacson shows the human possibilities of kindness and faith in the midst of hopelessness and fear. Perhaps what is most moving to students are the details of Judith's emerging sense of self as a woman. As she faces the developmental changes in her body, she is confronted with the barbaric regime of lack of privacy and forbidden modesty. The symbol of her femininity and careful preservation of her sexuality is characterized by the kerchief she uses to cover her shaven head. As she flirts with the Belgian mechanic and fantasizes about the French soldier, Judith mourns the loss of her dreams and future. Students should keep a careful account of her dreams, both real and fantastical. In discussion, the class can focus on how one preserves a dream in the midst of an uncertain future. How does Judith maintain her dream of attending the Sorbonne, and what dreams must she relinquish? What becomes a priority in terms of personal development?

When the SS guard screams at the young girls that there will be "no seed of Sarah,"[6] what implications does this hold for Judith as she boards the train for her final transport to Leipzig?

## Presentation Ideas

1. Personal testimony has become the most widely read literature of the Holocaust. Volumes have been published which detail the lives of Jews before, during, and after the war. Working in small groups, students should read several testimonies and choose one for class presentation. All students should be prepared to discuss the significant issues of these narrative pieces. Discussion can include an examination of the shared traditions, values, terrors, and human behaviors found in both *Seed of Sarah* and the chosen supplemental stories.

2. Create a map detailing the journey Judith and her family make from Hungary to Auschwitz-Birkenau to Leipzig and back to Hungary. The map should show the location of other concentration camps. Details of the route of annexation by the German army as well as the approach of the Allies could be included.

3. Students can work in small groups to research the basic mechanism of the German war machine. Using the following categories, each group should present a detailed account of how, when, and where Hitler created his plan for mass destruction of the Jews:
   - ▶ Wannsee Conference
   - ▶ The participation of the banks in confiscating personal property
   - ▶ Use of the rail system
   - ▶ Private business and its participation in the war effort
   - ▶ Hitler Youth Organization
   - ▶ Propaganda of the German government

Visual aids and films can be used to support the presentations.

### Writing Ideas

1. Judith Isaacson is faced with the reality of evil as part of human behavior. Using the genre of personal essay, students should write a narrative about a time in their life when they confronted the dark side of human behavior. Writing should include descriptive detail about time and place and reflect the emotional development of the writer as a result of this lesson. Encourage students to tell their stories in a narrative voice using dialogue, descriptive detail, and voice to show their message. This assignment can also be done in a fictional voice.

2. Read to the class the Ten Commandments from the Old Testament. Have students write a position paper on the commandment with the strongest message for them. Be sure to include specific detail explaining why and where this has an effect on their lives.

3. Write a narrative essay detailing a family tradition. Using a storytelling voice, students should focus on descriptive detail, color, sight, sound, and smell to define the traditional moment. In discovering the definition of family, have students focus on character development.

4. Judith Isaacson holds close to her heart the dream of one day attending the Sorbonne in Paris. Students should write a dream statement: What are their goals for the future? What and who have motivated them to pursue their dream? What must they do to make their dream become a reality? What obstacles stand in their way?

## Part Three: Liberation and Return

"Do oranges still exist?"[7]

The final unit of this book focuses on the American liberation of the camps, the freeing of the remaining prisoners and the rebuilding of lives from the ashes of the Holocaust. Students often find this section of Issacson's story the most disturbing. The detail of the forced marches, the fear of death, the sense of displacement, the lack of resources, and the realization of loss all create a picture of despair and hopelessness. With bombs exploding overhead and Germans desperately marching prisoners from one camp to the next, Judith faces the irony of being killed during the liberation efforts. "I watched, mesmerized, waiting to be engulfed by the approaching flames."[8] Isaacson examines the paradox of liberation in these closing chapters of the book, and yet she creates a picture of miraculous strength and hope and purpose. The students should focus their reading on the following concluding themes of the testimony:

▶ Defining freedom in the face of tragedy
▶ Issues of displacement: no family, no home, and no money
▶ Role of the American army in the relocation of Jews
▶ Fear: anti-Jewish riots, reprisals from the native population
▶ Immigration laws
▶ Strength, honor, and purpose

      In a moving account of her return to Europe, Isaacson takes the reader back to her home in Kaposvar following the war. Students should read carefully the details of this episode:

- ▶The despair in losing what one owned and cherished
- ▶The resentment and lies of the people in the town
- ▶The reality of human behavior as illustrated in the story about Dr. Biczó
- ▶The dream recaptured through the discovery of the items in the cellar cave
- ▶The rebuilding of a life with her "American Captain"
- ▶The journey from Europe to the United States: immigration laws

      Discussion should focus on the determination and resolve of this small family to survive and start over as a model of human behavior that gives profound contrast to the atrocities of the Holocaust.

## Part Four: The Return

"We cannot forget, but we must learn to forgive–from you." [9]

The final chapters of the book give a fascinating view of Isaacson's return to Eastern Europe in September of 1983. While doing research for her memoirs, Isaacson returns to Lichtenau and views the town's monument to the Jewish women who worked in the forced labor factories there. In March 1987 she is invited by the mayor to return and speak at a reunion of her former inmates. She is faced with not only the memories of her past, but with the tensions of a postwar Europe. The reading should focus on:

- ▶Political and social tensions existent in the towns of Eastern Europe
- ▶Growing anti-Semitism
- ▶Neo-Nazi groups
- ▶Identifying the culpable and the innocent
- ▶Forgiveness and remembrance

## Presentation Ideas

1. Just as Isaacson's book brings us to contemporary times, so can the research projects on this unit focus on political and historical events postwar. Students can be divided into small groups to research and present on the following topics:
   - ▶Immigration laws during the war and postwar: United States and Great Britain
   - ▶Prevalent anti-Semitism in Europe today
   - ▶Growth of the neo-Nazi movement
   - ▶War memorials
   - ▶War crimes: the Nuremberg Trials
   - ▶Current litigation: the Swiss Bank involvement in World War II, slave and forced labor claims, and insurance claims
2. The organization and relocation of displaced Jews was an extensive project for those who had survived the Holocaust. In the summer of 1945, Jews set up com-

munity organizations to address the issues present in their lives: finding homes, receiving counseling for trauma, medical assistance, and immigration. Students can research the following organizations to learn more of the fate of these survivors:

▶ The Central Council and the yearly council of the Congress of Liberated Jews

▶ The Zionist movement and the formation of a Jewish State of Israel

3. On November 20, 1945, the Nuremberg Trials began in Nuremberg, Germany. A court was established for examination of and punishment for crimes against humanity. Students should research the history and the events of these trials. Profiles of the accused can be examined and footage of the trials is available on film. (See Suggested Reading for support documents.)

## Writing Ideas

1. In personal essay form, students should write on the theme of forgiveness. They can focus on a specific event in their lives when they either forgave someone or were forgiven by someone for a wrong they committed against an individual.

2. Memory plays such a significant role in the lives of survivors: piecing together the scraps of their lives by storytelling, photographs, and contacts with other survivors. Writing on memory should be used extensively in the reading of these final chapters of *Seed of Sarah*. Have students begin with the words "I remember":

▶ . . . a time

▶ . . . a place

▶ . . . a feeling

▶ . . . when and where I saw (a person, an event, a place) for the first time/for the last time

▶ . . . when s/he (a characterization)

## Part Five: Examining Elements of Style

Judith Isaacson's book introduces students to the writing genre of personal testimony. Although a personal narrative, Isaacson employs the tone of an accurate observer: one who gives details in a factual voice, including dates, significant landmarks of historical events, and physical details of setting and events. In examining the style of this writing, it is important for students to recognize its journalistic approach. There are controlled elements in the book that use little metaphor or symbolism to show the story. What emerge are accounts of events in which emotions and reactions are woven into fact, distancing the reader somewhat from the events detailed. Teachers should pay close attention to the following events in the story and discuss with the students Isaacson's style and tone:

▶ The March Celebration in Kaposvar ( pp. 9–11)

▶ The call of Judith's father to the labor battalions (p. 25)

▶ Yom Kippur (p. 32)

▶Arrival at Auschwitz-Birkenau (p. 64)
▶Detail of Dr. Mengele (p. 86)
▶The approach of the Allies (p. 113)

An examination of style is most effective in comparison to other pieces of literature that use imagination and metaphor as the foundation of their story-telling. The chapter on *The Shawl*, by Cynthia Ozick, provides several comparative writing and discussion ideas on style and tone. (See page 98.)

## Suggested Reading:

Aichinger, Ilse. "Herod's Children." *Out of the Whirlwind: A Reader of Holocaust Literature*, Albert H. Friedlander, ed. New York: Schocken Books, New York, 1976.

Berenbaum, Michael and Abraham Peck, eds. *The Holocaust and History*. Bloomington and Indianapolis: Indiana University Press, 1998.

Chartock, Roselle and Jack Spencer. *The Holocaust Years: Society on Trial*. New York: Bantam Books, 1978.

Haas, Gerda. *These I Do Remember: Fragments from the Holocaust*. Freeport, Maine: The Cumberland Press, 1982.

Miller, Judith. *One by One: Facing the Holocaust*. Touchstone Book, New York: Simon and Schuster, 1990.

Ozick, Cynthia. *The Shawl*. New York: Vintage Books, 1990.

Ringelblum, Emmanuel. *Notes from the Warsaw Ghetto: The Journal of Emmanuel Ringelblum*. New York: Schocken Books, 1974, © 1958.

## Videography

*Nuremberg: Its Lesson for Today*, 76 minutes. Tinburger Institute. Distributed by Proto Books, Los Angeles.

*Nuremberg: Tyranny on Trial*. 50 minutes. Distributed by A & E.

[1] Judith Isaacson, *Seed of Sarah: Memoirs of a Survivor* (Chicago and Urbana: University of Illinois Press, 1991), p. 29.
[2] Ibid., p. 8.
[3] Ibid., p. 10.
[4] Ibid., p. 143.
[5] Ibid., p. 42.
[6] Ibid., p. 108.
[7] Ibid., p. 123.
[8] Ibid., p. 113.
[9] Ibid., p. 165.

# Night

Elie Wiesel. (New York: Bantam Books),1960. ISBN 0-553-27253-5.

## Glossary

**Cabbala.** A mystical doctrine of interpreting scripture through numerology, the meaning of letters of the alphabet, and words used by rabbis

**Deportation.** Forced exile

**Embark.** To depart or leave

**Entity.** A being, a form

**Firmament.** The heavens

**Hermetically sealed.** Airtight

**Iniquity.** Great wickedness or injustice

**Interlude.** A period of time between two actions or events

**Kapo.** From the Latin "capo" meaning "head"; a term used in the concentration camps and death camps to designate inmates who worked as functionaries of the camp; the kapos oversaw work detail and daily rituals of their fellow inmates and received privileges for their compliance with the Nazis

**Lamentation.** Mournful cry

**Nocturnal.** At night

**Pestilential.** Causing epidemic, disease

**Prostrate.** Cast down to the ground in humility or reverence

**Revelation.** God's manifestation to humankind

**Selection.** A process of separating the strong and young from the old and weak in the death camps

**Talmud.** A body of Jewish law that includes the commentaries on the Five Books of Moses

**Torah.** The Five Books of Moses

**Truncheon.** A powerful stick used to beat people

**Zionism.** A political movement among Jews to claim Palestine as the Jewish state

**Character List**
Eliezar Wiesel
His father
Moché the Beadle
Madame Schächter
Rabbi Eliahou
Akiba Drumer
Juliek

### Plot Summary

The fear of forgetting remains the main obsession for all those who have passed through the universe of the damned.[1]

*Night* is the account of the experiences of Elie Wiesel during the Holocaust. Written as an "imaginative autobiography,"[2] it is the story of Wiesel's life as a young boy in Sighet, Transylvania. Wiesel testifies to the horrors of his deportation to the concentration camps Auschwitz and later Buchenwald. The book details the struggle to maintain humanity, dignity in self, and faith in both God and man while surviving the terrifying conditions of life in the camps. With his father by his side, twelve-year-old Wiesel struggles to redefine his understanding of what the world has become.

### Objectives for Teaching *Night*

*Night* is a memoir rich in its investigation of Wiesel's emotional and spiritual journey during the Holocaust. Teachers should look carefully at the philosophical, moral, and ethical questions raised in the narrative and outlined in the following objectives:

▶ Understanding the life of a Hasidic Jew
▶ Defining faith
▶ The importance of questions
▶ Human potential: diminished and erased
▶ Survival in the concentration camps: fall from innocence
▶ Writing in a personal narrative genre

### Part One: In the Beginning

Lawrence Langer defines *Night* as "literature of atrocity" that transforms "gross horrors of the Holocaust to imaginative autobiography."[3] Wiesel's writing style artfully illuminates the initiation of a young boy into the reality of death and loss of faith. The story begins in the tone of a Talmudic parable with the opening line, "They called him Moché the Beadle. . . ."[4] The narrative starts a careful description of the life of young Wiesel in the small village of Sighet, Transylvania. In this tale, Wiesel catalogs the life of a Hasidic Jew. The voice of the boy is reverential in his description of family and community. Religious traditions abound, and high respect is paid to the elders and the rabbis of the community. With his education in the yeshiva, the religious school for Jewish boys, Elie is immersed in the grace and wonder of his God. Students should focus on the organization and structure of this community of scholars. It is a model for the best of human behaviors with its organized system of law and order. The rabbis act as spiritual and educational leaders. Fathers and sons share the traditions of the Five Books of Moses with their study and devotion to God. Keeping reading journals, students should record a portrait of a boy in this town of devout Jews. Writing should include discussion of the following questions:

▶ What are Elie's primary interests?

▶ How does he define his faith?

▶ How does Wiesel use his artful writing style to create this portrait of faith?

Also important in developing an understanding of the town is a close examination of the character Moché. Understanding the role of a beadle, the functional overseer of a congregation, helps the student understand this character; he organizes the service, prepares the necessary books and Torah scrolls for the rabbis, and keeps the sanctuary clean, safe, and protected. Moché also acts as a mentor when he initiates Elie's life of questioning with the words, "Man raises himself toward God with the questions he asks."[5] Thus the young boy engages in the study of the Cabbala with his teacher, searching for the mysteries of faith and devotion to the Supreme Being. At the deportation of Moché and the foreign Jews, Wiesel begins the shift from the solemnity and quiet of this community into a world of incomprehensible terror. Students should read aloud the story Moché tells upon his return and discuss the town's reaction. Focus questions might include:

▶ How is Moché perceived as an outsider after his return?

▶ What is the reaction of the community to his stories? Why the disbelief?

In a narrative voice, Wiesel introduces the surrounding historical events that begin to encroach upon this little community. As the laws of humanity are rewritten by the entrance of the Germans into Hungary, life begins to change for the community of Sighet. Through his storytelling, Wiesel filters in the historical significance of the approaching war. The Jews of Sighet remain optimistic about their futures, ignoring and justifying the war surrounding them. The reality of their situation gradually begins to impact on them. Students should take notes on the series of events that slowly change the perceptions of the elders and children of Sighet. Teachers should focus on the importance of the following details in the story:

▶The early infiltration and demeanor of the Germans in Sighet (p. 7)

▶The week of Passover: early sanctions and laws (p. 8)

▶The arrest of the leaders of the community (p. 8)

▶Establishing the ghettos (p. 9)

▶Establishing the Jewish Council, Jewish Police, and their significance to the community (p. 9)

▶Deportation (on the Sabbath) (p. 11)

As Elie is engaging in a life of questioning, the elders of the community are incapable of understanding the impending doom that is approaching. Students should keep notes on the reaction and words of the community leaders and be encouraged to discuss the difficult questions of the absence of resistance:

▶What prevented families from immigrating to safer lands?

▶How did the ghettoization of the Jews weaken them/make them stronger?

▶There is a pervasive air of confidence in the Germans in the town of Sighet. Why?

▶How do the people of Sighet cope with the fear and uncertainty of their future?

▶Wiesel writes of optimistic speeches and the pleasantries of waiting for deportation (p. 19). Students should record the tone of the author and examine the idea of absent anger and action.

It is of particular importance to examine the stylistic quality of these early chapters. Wiesel is aware of not only what story is being told, but how he is telling it. Students should be encouraged to look closely at the descriptive passages cataloging the incomprehensible changes that take place in Sighet. With attention to meticulous detail, Wiesel writes of the preparation for deportation, "Our back yard had become a real market place."[6] The descriptive detail of food, books, and personal possessions becomes an account that records the terror and anxiety of the events. The irony of a "blue sky" juxtaposed against "[the] littered . . . dusty ground"[7] creates a profound effect upon the reader. Other passages that should be analyzed for style and effect are:

▶The abandonment of homes (p. 14)

▶The description of the marketplace (p. 15)

▶The march to the "little ghetto" (p. 17)

▶The detail of the synagogue (p. 19)

## Part Two: Transformation: Physical, Emotional, Spiritual

Our eyes were opened, but too late.[8]

The historical, emotional, and philosophical ideas recorded in Wiesel's writing become truly significant upon his account of the deportation and concentration camp experience. *Night* is the originator of Holocaust literature using an imagistic style to create the harsh reality of the victims of the camps. The account of events in the camps and on the forced march becomes a multilayered story delin eating the cruelties of the physical hardships, the reality of the atrocious behavior of man, and the loss of spiritual fortitude and belief. Wiesel takes the reader on the journey with language that defines the incomprehensible. He reveals these three states of being with metaphor and exacting detail of an accurate observer using imagistic narrative. Each story written about his experience in the camps becomes a complex examination of thought, feeling, and reality. Students should pay close attention to the detail in examining the text not only for the emotional and historical effect, but also the stylistic manipulation of language, description, and use of metaphor. Journal work could reflect the following themes:

- ▶Reality versus disbelief
- ▶Human strength and weakness
- ▶Tradition and ritual: continuation and disintegration
- ▶Hope, memory, instinct

With the forced entrance into the cattle cars and the story of Madame Schächter, Wiesel begins the descent of his journey through the disbelief and terror of the camps. Leaving behind the close security of Sighet, the world of the Hasidic boy is completely altered. Each movement in the story takes the reader into the shock and innocence of this child as he tries to understand the atrocities of his experience. Wiesel uses the train to emphasize the effects of the Holocaust. The train becomes a metaphor for a "hermetically sealed" [9] coffin. As Madame Schächter envisions the fire of the ovens of Auschwitz, and all semblance of humanity begins to disappear in the confines of the cattle cars, the young Wiesel is already aware of the disappearance of his childhood. "I too had become a completely different person. The person of the Talmud, the child that I was, had been consumed in the flames." [10]

This early episode leads to the questioning that becomes the guide to this testimony. Elie is transformed into a bitter and frightened boy who begins to lose faith in the God who was once his guide to the mysteries of life. He is now faced with the terrifying and unbelievable horror of the SS and the kapos, plunging him into not only physical deprivation, but spiritual confusion as well. He says, "For the first time, I felt revolt rise up in me. Why should I bless His name? The Eternal, Lord of the Universe, the All-Powerful and Terrible, was silent. What had I to thank him for?" [11] This quote should lead the students into serious journal work. They should record and comment on the questions plaguing Elie's mind and soul. Listed below are a series of events from the story that will be the foundation for class discussion. Focus questions can be the prompts for journal writing and sharing during class:

- ▶What are the physical conditions of the camps?
- ▶Faith in humanity diminishes for Elie. What incidents alter his view of humanity?
- ▶How does instinct supplant spirituality? To what purpose?
- ▶How does Elie struggle with self-preservation versus the commitment to save his father?
- ▶Where do we hear the anger and cynicism in Wiesel's voice?

▶How does Wiesel use metaphor and artistic imagery to reveal the events of the camps?

▶How is hope diminished and replaced by fear?

▶What place do tradition and ritual have in a concentration camp?

In order to help focus on the emotional, spiritual, and physical transformation of Wiesel, it is important to have students pay close attention to the following scenes and ideas:

▶The significance of the "eight short, simple words" (p. 27) [12]

▶The irony of the camp motto (p. 38)

▶The words of admonishment by the inmate upon Elie's arrival at Auschwitz (p. 28)

▶The hanging of the young boy and three inmates and the significance of the metaphor of the soup (pp. 60–61)

▶Celebration of the Jewish New Year, Rosh Hashanah (p. 63)

▶The observance of Yom Kippur, the Day of Atonement (p. 65)

▶The loss of faith for Akiba Drumer and its effects on Elie (pp. 72–73)

▶Elie's surgery (pp. 74–76)

Students should read carefully these specific events from the text to help them gain a full experience of the concentration camps. Students may choose to keep a "quote" journal, recording the words of Wiesel that have lasting significance to them. (Suggestions for writing ideas about specific passages can be found in Writing Ideas.)

## Part Three: Between Father, Son, and God

And then I remembered that I had a father. [13]

The final chapters of *Night* focus on the evacuation and forced march to the concentration camp Buchenwald. These chapters examine the relationship between fathers and sons. From the very beginning, Elie makes a commitment to stay by his father's side no matter what the choices are. They survive the selections in the camps and share food, shelter, care, and morale. But the circumstances of the march take Elie into a world yet to be revealed to him: the disappearance of moral and ethical behavior between father and son and the extinguished respect and care given to an elderly loved one. As the head of the block advises Elie, "Don't forget you are in a concentration camp. Here, every man has to fight for himself and not think of anyone else. Even of his father. Here, there are no fathers, no brothers, no friends." [14] This statement shakes the very being of Elie who is faced with not only his own struggle to live, but his father's, also. Desperate and starving, Elie still makes a prayer to the God he believes has abandoned the Jews. He constantly questions the will of this same God. Students should record the changes in Eliel's demeanor during the march. Focus questions for journal work should follow the disintegration of Elie's faith in man and God:

▶How does physical necessity replace intellect and emotion?

▶What is the pact between Elie and his father? How and why is this pact challenged minute to minute during the march?

Specific scenes from the ending chapters hold the metaphoric and realistic imagery that takes the reader into the hell of the march. Philosophical questions about faith, hope, and God are intertwined into narratives of pain, loss, and disbelief. Students should take careful notes on the following scenes in order to gain a full understanding of the transformation between fathers and sons:

▶The story of Rabbi Eliahou and his son (p. 87)

▶The story of Juliek and the violin (p. 90)

▶The story of Meir Katz (pp. 97–98)

▶The death of Elie's father (pp.105–06)

After the death of his father, Elie says, "Nothing could touch me any more."[15] As the resistance movement takes over Buchenwald and aids in releasing the survivors, Elie emerges as a fifteen-year-old man forever changed by his experiences in the German concentration camps. The last lines of the book are, "From the depths of the mirror, a corpse gazed back at me. . . . The look in his eyes, as they stared into mine, has never left me."[16] The ending of *Night* is the beginning of a life that gives testimony to the injustices of the modern world. Research into the work of Wiesel since World War II is outlined in Writing Ideas.

## Presentation Ideas

1. Personal testimonies from Auschwitz-Birkenau abound. Have students work in small groups to research stories of survivors. Each group should be responsible for presenting the story in a creative and imaginative manner: a dramatic monologue, a play, a short story, a poem, or a web site. Students should include visual aids in their presentation: symbolic collage, maps, documents, and photographs. (See Suggested Reading for resources.)

2. In his writing and interviews, Elie Wiesel often refers to the story of Job from the Old Testament. Teachers should present this story to the class and have them write their analysis of the story. Questions they might consider:

   ▶How does the story of Job have significance in terms of the Holocaust?

   ▶Does Wiesel identify with Job as an individual?

   ▶How are the questions of faith for Job similar/different from Wiesel's?

3. The prophet Elijah (Eliahou the Prophet) has particular significance in the lives of the Jewish people. Students should reread the section from *Night* about Eliahou and his son and research the Old Testament story of Elijah. Students could write on the following ideas:

   ▶Why does Elijah the prophet have such significance to the Jewish people?

   ▶What is the connection between the teachings of Elijah and the plight of the Jews in the concentration camps?

4. Many survivors have recorded the forced marches of the Jews from the eastern camps further into Germany. Students could research stories of the marches from other survivors to share in class. A group could be responsible for creating a map illustrating the paths of the marches.

5. Wiesel writes briefly at the end of *Night* about the resistance movement within the concentration camp. Students should research the resistance movement in Auschwitz. Questions they should discuss:
> ▶ How was the movement organized?
> ▶ To what extent did the resistance help the victims within the camps?
> ▶ What outside resources did the resistance members have? Who supported their efforts?

6. Wiesel has emerged from the Holocaust an influential speaker on world issues of human rights. Small groups could research the work of Wiesel since the war. (See Suggested Reading for Nobel Prize speech reference.) Questions they should address:
> ▶ How has Wiesel become the voice of *Shoah*? (Hebrew for remembrance)
> ▶ How does his writing reflect his views on current events?

To supplement this activity, students should keep a two-week journal on current events in regard to human rights. Newspaper clippings should be saved and presented to the class.
> ▶ What areas of the world are suffering under the oppression of a ruling force?
> ▶ Where are problems of human rights existent in our own country?
> ▶ How and where is Wiesel still letting his voice be heard?

7. Numerous artists of the camps depicted the darkness of their physical and emotional experiences. Students could research a specific artist of the Holocaust and give a presentation on art as symbol and meaning. (See chapter on Art of the Holocaust.)

## Writing Ideas

1. The writing of Elie Wiesel has provided the world with a full vocabulary and imagery of the Holocaust. Students should keep a "Quote Journal" writing down the quotes with the most significance to them. They should respond to their reaction and feelings about these quotes in personal writing.

2. Wiesel says, "Never shall I forget. . . ." [17] and the significance of memory becomes the foundation of Holocaust writing. Students should write a series of personal essays based on the idea of memory or remembrance. Each piece could begin with the words: I remember . . . (a time, place, feeling). Students may also write with the prompt: I do not remember a time when I. . . . Students should be encouraged to use descriptive language to tell their personal stories. This is a good assignment for poetry, also.

3. Students could organize a debate on the role of the United States as the watchdog of human rights. Questions they might address:
> ▶ What is the responsibility of the United States government where acts of aggression are perpetrated on innocent victims in foreign countries?
> ▶ How should the government support these areas of unrest? Military action? Diplomacy?
> ▶ What are our responsibilities as individuals about these disturbing events?
> ▶ What issues of prejudice are present in our own society? How do we address them?

4. The idea of choice, or lack of it, is a predominant issue in the lives of the concentration camp victims. Students should keep a journal about the choices, both emotional and physical, Elie is forced to make. As a creative writing assignment, students could write a short story about the theme of choice, creating characters faced with difficult choices in their lives. They may also write in personal essay form about a time in their lives when they were forced to make a difficult choice.

5. The closing lines of *Night* show Elie looking into a mirror, unable to recognize himself. Students should create a "self-portrait" that symbolizes who they are at this point in their lives. The project should involve the visual arts: collage, computer graphics, drawing, painting, bookmaking, sculpture. A supplemental "museum catalogue" should accompany the artwork with biographical data, a discussion of medium, and the artist's interpretation of his/her work.

## Suggested Reading

Abrahamson, Irving. *Against Silence: The Voice and Vision of Elie Wiesel.* Vol. 3, ed., Holocaust Library, 1995.

Adler, David. *We Remember the Holocaust.* New York: Henry Holt and Company, 1989.

Arad, Yitzhak. "The Armed Jewish Resistance in Eastern Europe," *The Holocaust and History.* Michael Berenbaum and Abraham Peck, eds. Bloomington and Urbana: Indiana Press, 1998.

*Fortunoff Video Archive for Holocaust Testimony.* Garland Reference Library of Social Science, 604. New York: Garland Publishing, 1990.

Haas, Gerta. *These I Do Remember: Fragments from the Holocaust.* Freeport, Maine: The Cumberland Press, 1982.

Langer, Lawrence. *Holocaust Testimonies.* New Haven: Yale University Press, 1991.

Leitner, Isabelle and Irving Leitner. *From Auschwitz to Freedom.* New York: Anchor Books, 1978.

Levi, Primo. *Survival in Auschwitz.* New York: Collier Books, reprint, 1987.

Wiesel, Elie. *All Rivers Run to the Sea: An Audio Cassette.* New York: Random House Audio.

_____. Nobel Peace Prize Acceptance Speech. Elie Wiesel. Dec. 10, 1986.

_____. *Souls on Fire: Portraits and Legends of Chasidic Masters.* New York: Vintage Press, 1973.

[1] Elie Wiesel, "Why Would I Write: Making No Become Yes" (*New York Times Book Review*, I Section 7, Column 1, April 14, 1985), p. 13.

[2] Lawrence Langer, *The Holocaust and the Literary Imagination* (New London: Yale University Press, 1975), p. 92.

[3] Ibid., p. 31.

[4] Elie Wiesel, *Night* (New York: Bantam Books, 1960), p. 1.

[5] Ibid., p. 2.

[6] Ibid., p. 13.

[7] Ibid.

[8] Ibid., p. 21.

[9] Ibid., p. 22.

[10] Ibid., p. 34.

[11] Ibid., p. 31.

[12] Ibid., p. 27.

[13] Ibid., p. 101.

[14] Ibid., p. 105.

[15] Ibid., p. 107.

[16] Ibid., p. 109.

[17] Ibid., p. 32.

Books

# This Way for the Gas, Ladies and Gentlemen ———

Tadeuz Borowski, translated by Barbara Vedder (New York: Penguin Book), 1967.
ISBN 0-14-0812624-7.

## Character List
Tadek
Henri the Frenchman
Mrs Haneczksa
Ivan

## Plot Summary

But how did it happen that you survived?[1]

*This Way for the Gas, Ladies and Gentlemen,* by Tadeuz Borowski, is a disturbing and provocative account of a man's experiences in Auschwitz-Birkenau death camp. Using first-person narrative, Borowski creates a piece of literature that teeters on the fine line between personal testimony and fiction. With his own experience in the camps as the foundation for his writing, the author tells the story of Tadek, a prisoner who acts as a functionary of the camp. The functionaries, like the kapos of the camps, work for the Nazis. The kapos organize and command the functionaries, and they both hope for a bit of privilege for their labors: more food, bartering objects, and clothing. The story shows the routine of camp life that offers no hope or sympathy for the victims of the Holocaust. Borowski examines the mutual responsibility and participation in the camp's atrocities by the prisoners who worked in the crematoria, at the train transports, and in the labor camps. In his eloquent introduction, Jan Kott says, "The book is one of the cruelest of testimonies to what men did to men, and a pitiless verdict that anything can be done to a human being."[2] The stories look carefully at the tenuous distinction between victim and executioner. Borowski considers the prospect of survival after the liberation of the camps in view of these moral and emotional conflicts.

Because this collection of short stories contains autobiographical material, the close connection of the narrator's voice and Borowski's is one that requires careful study. It is suggested that students read the brief introduction and several of Borowski's poems to gain a complete understanding of this book. (See Suggested Reading for resources.)

## Objectives for Teaching *This Way for the Gas, Ladies and Gentlemen*

The content of this book is both disturbing and thought provoking for young readers. It is unusual for readers to experience testimony in which the behavior and participation of the camp inmates is questioned, but Borowski provides a multilayered view of human behavior that makes clear human nature is complex and indefinable. Teachers should focus discussion on the moral and ethical dilemmas and the ideas of choice and responsibility created by the atrocities of the camps.

The short stories contain shared themes that are developed and examined in every piece. The following are the themes to be examined:
- The multiple voices of the narrator
- The style and form of writing used to reflect the voices
- The ethical and emotional difficulty of being a survivor
- Life after liberation

## Part One: Listening to the Voices

### The Voice of the Functionary

So Sosnowiec-Bedzin was a good rich transport. [3]

The first-person narrator's voice lays the foundation upon which Borowski builds the complex ideas and feelings of the short stories. In the first story "This Way for the Gas, Ladies and Gentlemen," Borowski explores the layers of experience of the functionaries at the camps. It is important for students to have a clear understanding of the camp's workings and organization. Tadek, the main character throughout the collection of stories, is a Polish laborer who has been imprisoned because of the political views expressed in his writings. The reader is introduced to the voice of objective, unemotional documentation with the creation of this character who mirrors the experiences of Borowski. Tadek is a worker, simply performing a function that will ultimately aid in his own survival. As a member of the team that unloads the transports, he details the horror of the deportees with a factual, dispassionate voice.

The "functionary" voice is created through the use of meticulous documentation of the camp's events. The first story begins with the detail of the efficiency of the delousing. With the lack of emotion that characterizes this narrator's voice, the nakedness, heat, marching, and herding is related without judgment or reaction. As the men in Tadek's battalion prepare to unload an incoming transport of Jews, Borowski provides the reader with the elemental organization of the death camp Auschwitz-Birkenau. We become aware of the food distribution, marching regime, transport arrivals, and work crews. As Tadek describes, "A cheerful little station, very much like any other provincial railway stop,"[4] Borowski delivers the horror of the story's events. The daily routine of unloading the thousands of prisoners becomes a catalog of the possessions, a cursory view of the people, and a cruel and emotionless accounting of the murder of innocent victims. With admiration for the order and efficiency of the action of the crews and

Books

officers, Tadek's voice represents the numbness and loss of human compassion by those who struggle to survive at any cost. Their inhumanity is a result of the cruelty and horror inflicted upon them. They learn to be cruel at the hands of their oppressors.

The style of this voice reveals the intent of the author. Students should look carefully at the passages of "lists" on pages 37–38 and 42. Borowski gives witness to the horror of unloading the trains through Tadek's detailed account of his job: "We climb inside. In the corners amid human excrement and abandoned wristwatches lie squashed, trampled infants, naked little monsters with enormous heads and bloated bellies. We carry them out like chickens, holding several in each hand."[5] This atrocity is delivered with a journalistic accounting, a documentary voice which allows no room for reflection on responsibility or shame. This is the voice of a survivor—one that will do anything to make it into the next hour alive.

Borowski masterfully crafts the combination of horror and routine. He gives voice to the part of the human soul that is lost because of the atrocities of the Holocaust. Students should keep a reading journal throughout the collection, making note of this "functionary" voice of Tadek and his fellow inmates. The following questions should be considered in relation to this voice:

▶ How is the importance of food the foundation for participation in the functionary role?
▶ How does Borowski give historical reference by noting the numbers of victims in the camps?
▶ What is the "normal" routine for processing new arrivals? What makes a "good" transport?
▶ What is the code of ethics established by the workers when handling the inmates' goods and possessions? What are the German rules of order in sorting the goods?

## The Voice of Anger and Cynicism

"One hears all kind of talk, and dammit, they'll run out of people!"[6]

The cruelties forced upon these functionaries and their horrifying behavior creates a new persona of man. Borowski writes with a startling intensity in a voice hardened by cynicism, anger, and bitter irony. The anger and passion that the kapos and functionaries should feel toward their captors would endanger their own lives, so in a frightening twist of character these men turn upon themselves and their fellow prisoners. Students will find these passages difficult to understand and discussion should include the paradox of this camp behavior: victim and executioner becoming indistinguishable from each other. While reading for this voice, students should take accurate notes in their journals of the events that precede and follow the description and declarations of anger and fury expressed by the prisoners. They should consider what prompts this anger and what purpose it serves in their struggle to survive.

The voice of cynicism includes complaints about the "quality" of the transports, the passivity of the arriving prisoners, the prejudice against the different ethnic groups in the camp, the deceit that exists between the functionaries, and the system of power among themselves. Borowski paints these men as replicas of the Germans who imprison them. With a total lack of moral and ethical behavior surrounding them, the kapos and workers are reduced to the same level of human behavior as their captors: monstrous, cruel, atrocious, murderous. Students should think about the following questions:

▶ How and why is this angry voice directed toward the inmates?

▶ How is this anger a protective device that keeps the workers alive?

▶ How are the voices of the workers and the German guards barely distinguishable from one another?

Students should consider the following quotes and passages in expressing this anger and cynicism:

▶ "They can't run out of people, or we'll starve to death in this blasted camp. All of us live on what they bring."[7]

▶ "Religion is the opium of the people. . . . If they didn't believe in God and eternal life, they'd have smashed the crematoria long ago."[8]

▶ "It is the camp law: people going to their death must be deceived to the very end. This is the only permissible form of charity."[9]

▶ "Look at the Greeks, they know how to make the best of it! They stuff their bellies with anything they find."[10]

This tone of bitter cynicism makes itself apparent throughout the collection and should be carefully noted and discussed.

## The Voice of Compassion and Fear

It is impossible to control oneself any longer.[11]

Hidden deep below the voices of documentation and anger is a small voice of fear, compassion, and despair. Borowski gives brief and riveting lines to Tadek who suffers at his own behavior. It is through this voice that a tiny glimpse of humanity leaks out and the complexity of the character develops. Not completely untouched by his life at Auschwitz, Tadek struggles to repress his fear and disgust. Through careful examination of this voice, the reader sees the terrible legacy of guilt and despair that will emerge for the survivors after liberation. The voice is compassionate and nostalgic and gives testimony to the true man.

Attention to the following passages will reveal the significance of this voice:

▶ "I tie a piece of rope around the suitcase where the onion and tomatoes [come] from my father's garden in Warsaw. . . ."[12]

▶ "They are the ones who had been ordered to step to the right—the healthy and the young who will go to the camp. In the end they too will not escape death."[13]

▶ "I am terribly tired."[14]

► "I am not sure if all of this is actually happening, or I am dreaming.
► There is a humming inside my head. I feel that I must vomit."[15] "My head swims, my legs are shaky, again, I feel like throwing up."[16]
► "And over there is the gas chamber; communal death, disgusting and ugly."[17]

Discussion should focus on what emotions become apparent when Tadek reveals this vulnerable voice within him. Students should consider why the women and children elicit the most heartrending confessions from Tadek. As Tadek weakens and finds it intolerable to unload yet another transport, his friend Henri protects him from the German soldiers. His weakness of emotion will prove to make his survival in the camps almost impossible.

### The Voice of Appreciation of the Natural World

Mixed within this voice of sorrow and despair, Borowski portrays Tadek as a man of poetic sensibilities. He loves nature and beauty and searches for the smallest evidence there is still something worth looking at in this barbed-wire world. It is through this voice that the lyricism of Borowski as a poet becomes apparent. In his descriptions of the heat (p. 37), sunsets (pp. 45, 49), and the beautiful woman who descends from the train (p. 44), Borowski reveals the humanity that still flickers within Tadek. Each of the stories in this collection gives evidence of this poetic voice and should be carefully noted by the students. Through the creation of these beautiful passages, Borowski proves a human being still exists amidst the horrors of the camp. There is an inner self that surpasses the cruel and relentless behavior of the worker Tadek.

In the stories ending the collection, there is yet another voice to consider: defeat and total despair. This narrator's voice will be discussed in Part Five.

### Part Two: A "Normal" Day in Auschwitz-Birkenau

#### "A Day at Harmenz"

"Today there's going to be a selection in the camp."[18]

Having established the characters and definition of life in the camps in the first story, Borowski uses the story "A Day at Harmenz" to illustrate the terror and cruelty of one twenty-four-hour period in the life of a prisoner. The story is written in seven short episodes. Although all of the horror of the camp is experienced in only one day, the seven stories comprise the metaphor of seven days in a week, reinforcing the idea of routine, cycles, and never-ending experience. The range of feelings in these interconnected stories is devastating in its sheer magnitude of fear. Tadek faces in one day betrayal, loss, anger, revenge, violence, and death. The story is very similar to the personal testimony of Alexander Solzhenitsyn's *One Day in the Life of Ivan Denisovich*, a story unrelenting in its definition of what is "normal" in a concentration camp. (See Suggested Reading.)

Each story has its own important message for the reader and introduces a different perspective on the prisoners' lives in the camps. Borowski maintains the variety of voices represented by Tadek in the first story while delivering the impact of the day's experiences. In teaching these vignettes, teachers could assign students to be responsible for the presentation of each story. Students should be able to discuss what is the most important element of plot in each vignette (indicated by roman numerals) as well as the significance of the events of the stories. Using dramatic monologues, scene re-enactment, and quote analysis, students should use the following questions as guides in understanding the story's impact:

**I**

▶ Who is Mrs Haneczka and what role does the black market play in life at the camps?

▶ How are the cruelties of the officers and guards mirrored in the behavior of the prisoners?

▶ Where do you see the conflict between self-responsibility and survival? What choices does Tadek make in order to survive?

▶ What is the significance of Becker's history? Discuss the quote: "Real hunger is when one man regards another man as something to eat."[19]

**II**

▶ How does this story detail the relationship between the guards, kapos, and prisoners?

▶ Why does Tadek's singing endanger his life? What threat does he now have to face?

**III**

▶ As he passes in and out of the camp, Tadek observes the little girl who is the daughter of the Unterscharführer (camp leader). What is disturbing about this image?

▶ What is the importance of Tadek's personal possessions of a watch and good shoes?

▶ How does the incident with the soap "Warsaw" become an event of life and death?

**IV**

▶ Who is the character Janek? What does he represent in the camp?

**V**

▶ What are the implicit rules of eating?

▶ What is the kapo's reaction to Tadek's giving his soup away?

**VI**

▶ What news of the outside world filters into the camps? What fears or hopes does this arouse in the prisoners?

**VII**

▶ This story brings together Mrs Haneczka, Ivan, the kapo, Becker, and Tadek. How does the end confirm the tragedy and terror of all of their lives?

▶ Tadek's voice of compassion and defeat ends this story. Where do you hear it?

In considering the important elements of this story, the students should also research the significant references to the natural world. The haunting and beautifully lyrical description of the chestnut trees, stars, raspberry bushes, and trees beyond the barbed wire give voice to the appreciation of the beauty of the world despite the hardships of the camps.

## Part Three: A "Normal" Life

### "The People Who Walked On"

> Between two throw-ins in a soccer game, right behind my back,
> three thousand people had been put to death.[20]

Borowski distinguishes himself as a Holocaust writer who uses the minimalist style to reveal the horror of the camps. There is a reductive quality to the writing with its descriptive passages, anecdotal detail, and brutal frankness. The opening section of this story details the building of a soccer field. Borowski gives the character Tadek an opportunity to exercise his voice of appreciation for beauty and life amidst the ruins of man's inhumanity to man. Students should read these passages listening for the passion and will to live that exist in Tadek. The author alternates detail as quickly as the passing of the ball, and the pace of the writing reflects the speed of the moment: the playing and the extermination of a new transport arrival. "I returned with the ball and kicked it back inside the field. It traveled from one foot to another and, in a wide arc, returned to goal. I kicked it towards a corner. Again it rolled out into the grass. Once more I ran to retrieve it. But as I reached down, I stopped in amazement—the ramp was empty."[21] This writing delivers shock and despair in abrupt, blunt blows, much like the physical abuse perpetrated by the kapos and guards. It illustrates an ironic seesaw of comradery and normalcy versus violence and destruction.

The entire story is a series of anecdotes juxtaposing the "normalcy" of camp life versus atrocity. Students should examine this seesaw of emotion in the following detail:

- ▶ The efficiency of the Auschwitz post office versus the barbarity of the availability of only one hypodermic needle (p. 84)
- ▶ The news of the landing of the Allies versus the flame-filled night sky from the crematoria (p. 85)
- ▶ The beauty of the birth of a child in the women's lager versus the degradation of the whorehouse (p. 89)
- ▶ The concerts and nightly entertainment versus the procession of new arrivals to the gas chamber (p. 94)

"The People Who Walked On" is also a testament to the constant asking of unanswerable questions. Students should look at the significance of the following questions posed by the characters in the story:

- ▶ "What could have made it so sick so suddenly?"[22]
- ▶ "But if a man does evil, he'll be punished, won't he?"[23]

▶ "What can you do if they fall all over themselves to get to the gas?" [24]

▶ "Will evil be punished? I mean in human, normal terms?" [25]

Students should make careful note of the historical references made in this chapter to the approaching allies and defeat of the Germans. When the gates of Auschwitz-Birkenau are opened by the liberators to reveal the horror inside the camp, the significance of these questions gains a different perspective.

## "Auschwitz, Our Home (A Letter)"

> You have no idea what a vast expanse can fit between the frames of one small window. [26]

Asking questions about punishment and evil leads Borowski to the final section of this book where self-responsibility poses the most difficult questions of all. With the slow descent into the hell of Auschwitz, Borowski guides the reader into the anguish and defeat of Tadek. This story gives an interesting juxtaposition of the "inside world" of Auschwitz versus the "outside" world of Warsaw. This theme of inside/outside also acts as a metaphor for Borowski's psychological state. While Tadek observes the physical plant of the camp, the roads, barbed wire, watch towers, bunks, and buildings, he takes the reader on an interior tour of his past life. Written as a letter to his lover, who is imprisoned in the adjoining Birkenau death camp, Tadek reveals a nostalgic, anecdotal voice that rings with the style of the poet within him. The interior view of his memory shows his love of home, family, poetry, German literature, music, and philosophy. He recalls the sky of Warsaw, his lover's smell, the sensuality of wilting flowers. He tells his lover "I smile and think that one human being must always be discovering another— through love." [27] Students should make an outline of opposing images presented in these nine vignettes, detailing this declaration of love versus the threat of death through extermination. The following themes give evidence to the struggle for life against death:

▶ Dancing versus the traffic to the gas chamber (p. 112)

▶ The "entertainment" of the camps versus imminent starvation and death (pp. 117–18)

▶ Training to be an orderly versus emptying the trains of dead babies (p. 116)

Students should read carefully the passage on pages 121–22. In a thoughtful and disturbing voice, Tadek ponders the future of hope and a normal life. He contemplates the process survivors will have to go through to recreate families and relationships. Students should consider the following questions in relation to these final pages of this story:

▶ What are his hopes for the "rights of man"? [28]

▶ What effect does hope have on the prisoners when viewing their fate?

▶ For what does Tadek have hope?

▶ What is the "concentration camp mentality"? [29]

Books

The ending of the story prepares the reader for the decay that slowly begins to dissolve the resolve of the functionaries and Tadek. Students should consider the change in tone in the narrator's voice.

▶How are the ironies of the camp affecting Tadek now?
▶How do the memories of Warsaw and the news from his brother weaken his resolve to survive?

## Part Four: The Descent into Self

### The Death of Schillinger
### The Man with the Package
### The Supper
### A True Story

As the author leads the reader to the deepest recesses of Tadek's psyche, he is unrelenting in the detail of the extermination process of the camp. For every thought of hope or introspection from Tadek, Borowski delivers a brutal description of violence and horror. "The Death of Schillinger" profiles First Sergeant Schillinger. He is the Nazi prototype of a good officer: tough, unwavering in his resolve, organized, and brutal. For a brief moment, Borowski allows the reader to triumph in the death of this man, but immediately responds with the voice of the functionary. The narrator remarks on the triumph of the kapos and workers to take command of the situation and "drive them [the prisoners] right into the gas chamber."[30] Mirroring the experiences of the prisoners in the camps, Borowski leaves no room for contemplation or triumph. Over the screams of the dying Schillinger, we hear the screams from the gas chamber and are reminded there is no equity in these deaths.

"The Man with the Package," "A True Story," and "Silence" continue with this voice of descending hope. Students should note the increased tone of despair and defeat. The following quotes could be used for small-group discussion, writing prompts, or presentations to the class.

▶"Holding a package would be like holding someone's hand. . . ."[31]
▶". . . [A] Jew from Estonia tried to convince me that human brains are, in fact, so tender you can eat them absolutely raw."[32]
▶"Don't tell me any more stories."[33]

These stories reveal the voice within Tadek that begins to question his survival. Contemplation and reflection are the underpinnings of this voice and the documentary voice is mixed with regret and fear.

## Part Five: The Future through the Past
### Silence
### The January Offensive
### A Visit

These three stories offer a view of life during and after liberation, culminating in the final story of the collection. In these stories Borowski begins to ask the moral and ethical questions that arise after liberation. Having lived years with starvation, cold, hard labor, and death, the functionaries must begin to examine the code of behavior that allowed them to survive. With the entry of the American officer into the barracks, the workers are faced with their first view of civilized behavior. As the officer assures the men justice will be served, the reader becomes aware these men have no context in which to understand his pleas for lawfulness. The philosophical dilemma of how one immediately abandons the lawlessness of the camps for moral behavior is an absurdity, and Borowski illustrates this with the brutal murder of the hidden kapo.

"The January Offensive" is a play on words describing the problems the survivors faced after liberation. The survivors must now defend themselves against the prejudice of the Germans, the successful businessmen, and wealthy citizens. These people who did not suffer the terrors of the camps scorn the poverty and "weaknesses" of the survivors. The offensive is against those who did not suffer the cruelties of the camps. In detailing the conditions of the displaced persons camps and the absurdity of trying to start a "normal life," Borowski reveals a voice of frustration and fear. This story recounts the reality of Borowski's return to Poland. Surrounded by poets and philosophers, the survivors wrangle over politics and human nature. Students should read carefully the passages on page 168 that detail the dialogue of the survivors. In Tadek's voice we see the pain of recreating a life. Tadek states: "We believe neither in the morality of man nor in the morality of the systems."[34] As the Russians take over Poland with promises of freedom, once again the people are repressed and frustrated in their dreams and desires. The prospects of escaping to the capitalistic west or working with the new government of Poland to establish a free society fade with the corruption of the leaders. It is important that students have an understanding of the eventual descent of the Russians upon Poland and the establishment of the iron curtain following the war. (See Suggested Reading.)

Students should read these chapters and be prepared to discuss the moral and ethical choices survivors had to make upon regaining their freedom. In "A Visit," how does Borowski illustrate the memories of the human bodies, the fire of the crematoria, the labor, and the starvation follow Tadek into the life he must now lead? This story relates how Borowski understands that as a survivor the hardest task is still ahead—to look inside himself: "I am troubled by one persistent thought—that I have never been able to look also at myself. A certain young poet, a symbolic-realist, says with a certain flippant sarcasm that I have a concentration camp mentality."[35] With this frightening self-reality, Borowski takes us into the final story of the book.

## The World of Stone
*This Way for the Gas, Ladies and Gentlemen* offers no hope to the reader in the concluding story. Here we do not see families reuniting, immigration to the free world, a new life reborn. Instead, Borowski leads the reader to the horror of surviving with the despair and guilt of the inmates' behavior in the camps. Using

metaphor to define the state of mental anguish Tadek is suffering, Borowski paints a picture of a man "like a foetus in a womb, a terrible knowledge had been ripening inside me and filling my soul with foreboding."[36] This foreboding is the emptiness of feeling, the depression of survival, the disappointment in the future, and the terror of memory. Students should listen to this new voice of lack of feeling. The lethargy and indifference is characterized by the flatness of the tone, the lack of color in the detail, and the heaviness of the imagery. Students should record in a list the words that characterize this voice: there is no joy or appreciation of "the simple life" for which Tadek longed in the camps. Understanding that feeling has left him, Tadek resolves "to write with great intellectual effort [to] grasp the significance of the events, things and people I have seen."[37] We are left with this moving collection of stories that documents his loss of life as a result of the Holocaust.

### Presentation Ideas:

1. Dividing the students into small groups, students could research and prepare a debate on the following questions:
    ▶ Is there a standard of morality in the world?
    ▶ Does the definition of what is moral change with time?
    ▶ Does our moral system in the United States differ from other countries?
    ▶ Does the challenge of survival amend the moral code? In what circumstances?

    Teachers could provide a hypothetical situation of a moral choice a young person might face as a foundation for this debate.
2. The war machine of Nazi Germany was supported in part by the labor-camp workers. Students should research the role of major businesses that used the prisoners for labor. A profile of these companies could be presented to the class. Suggestions for specific businesses: I. G. Farben and Mercedes. (See Suggested Reading.)
3. Students could each research a poem that defines a moment of beauty. Oral recitation and presentation of the poem's author and ideas could accompany the research.
4. Students should work in small groups to create a document of the "Rights of Humankind." This document could have an artistic presentation and be created in poster form to be displayed in the classroom and school.
5. Detention camps were initially organized for political dissidents. Students should research these camps and discover how these detention camps became early models for the death camps. How did the Nazis transform "detention" into "extermination"?
6. Borowski details the "entertainment" that took place in the camps. Students should research the theater, art, and music that was created and presented in the concentration camps. Videos and art books provide a multitude of images and sounds with support from the Internet with its interactive audio. (See chapters on Music of the Holocaust and Art of the Holocaust.)

### Writing Ideas

Because this novel is presented as a series of short stories, writing ideas are presented in sequential reference to the themes of the short stories.

1. The voice of the survivor is one shared by many Holocaust survivors. Students should read the passages from Isaacson's *Seed of Sarah* where she refuses the privileges of being a kapo in order to uphold her moral and ethical standards. Wiesel also examines self-responsibility in *Night* as he is confronted with the choice of his survival or staying with his father. In Hegi's *Stones from the River*, the main character Trudi risks her own life to rescue Jews attempting to flee the Nazis. These characters and testimonies all provide background information for a discussion on Tadek's behavior. Students should read these excerpts and write a response journal considering the following questions:

    ▶ How is the responsibility of choice a shared Holocaust experience for these authors?

    ▶ How do these authors define the rules for survival?

2. Students should make a list of the many "voices" they use in their everyday lives. They should consider their voices as students, siblings, children, and friends. Accompanying this list could be a paragraph describing these voices: What are the different tones? What experiences elicit these voices? After "listening" carefully to themselves, students could choose from the following ideas:

    ▶ Write a short story in which the main character has a similar voice to your own. Using a narrative style, detail the reaction to a particular experience of the main character that reflects this voice.

    ▶ Create an artistic representation of one of the voices of Tadek. Consider what art medium would best express the voice of the functionary, anger and cynicism, beauty and despair. A companion piece reflecting this voice within you should accompany this presentation.

3. The following is a poem written by Tadeuz Borowski after the war. Teachers should use this poem to gain insight into the survivor's plight after liberation.

### The Sun of Auschwitz

You remember the sun of Auschwitz
And the green of the distant meadows, lightly
Lifted to the clouds by birds
no longer green in the clouds,
but seagreen white. Together
we stood looking into the distance and felt
the far away green of the meadows and the clouds'
seagreen white within us,
as if the color of the distant meadows
were our blood or the pulse
beating within us, as if the world
existed through us and nothing changed
as long as we were there. I remember
your smile as elusive
as a shade of the color of the wind,
a leaf trembling on the edge
of sun and shadow, fleeting
yet always there. So you are
for me today, in the seagreen
sky, the greenery and
the leaf-rustling wind. I feel
you in every shadow, every movement,
and you put the world around me
like your arms. I feel the world
as your body, you look into my eyes
and call me with the whole world.[38]

—Tadeuz Borowski

The following questions can be used as a guide for the reading and discussion of the poem:
- ▶ Who is the speaker in the poem?
- ▶ What images does Borowski use to create the "outside world" beyond Auschwitz? What does the repetition of the word "green" imply?
- ▶ To whom is this poem addressed?
- ▶ The word "sun" could have two meanings in this poem. What are they?
- ▶ What is the feeling of this poem?

## Suggested Reading

Abzug, Robert H. *Inside the Vicious Heart: Americans and the Liberation of Nazi Concentration Camps.* New York: Oxford University Press, 1985.

*Against Forgetting. Twentieth Century Poetry of Witness.* Carolyn Forché, ed. New York: W. W. Norton & Company,1993.

Borkin, Joseph. *The Crime and Punishment of I. G. Farben.* New York: Free Press, 1978.

Brogan, Patrick. *The Captive Nations: Eastern Europe: 1945–1990.* New York: Avon Books, 1990.

Des Pres, Terence. *The Survivor: An Anatomy of Life in the Death Camps.* New York: Pocket Books, 1976.

Hillesum, Etty. *An Interrupted Life: The Diaries of Etty Hillesum.* Translated from the Dutch by Arno Pomerans. New York: Pantheon Books, 1983; Washington Square Press, 1985.

Levi, Primo. *Survival in Auschwitz: The Nazi Assault on Humanity.* Translated from the Italian by Stuart Woolf. New York: Orion, 1959; Collier Books, 1986.

Solzhenitsyn, Alexander. *One Day in the Life of Ivan Denisovich.* New York: Signet Classics, 1998.

---

[1] Tadeuz Borowski, *This Way for the Gas, Ladies and Gentlemen*, translated by Barbara Vedder (New York: Penguin Books, 1976), p. 22.

[2] Ibid., p. 12.

[3] Ibid., p. 49.

[4] Ibid., p. 33.

[5] Ibid., p. 39.

[6] Ibid., p. 31.

7 Ibid.

8 Ibid., p. 32.

9 Ibid., p. 37.

10 Ibid., p. 40.

11 Ibid., p. 42.

12 Ibid., p. 32.

13 Ibid., p. 38.

14 Ibid., p. 40.

15 Ibid., p. 41.

16 Ibid., p. 43.

17 Ibid., p. 44.

18 Ibid., p. 55.

19 Ibid., p. 54.

20 Ibid., p. 84.

21 Ibid., p. 83.

22 Ibid., p. 89.

23 Ibid., p. 90.

24 Ibid., p. 91.

25 Ibid., p. 97.

26 Ibid., p. 101.

27 Ibid., p. 110.

28 Ibid., p. 121.

29 Ibid., p. 122.

30 Ibid., p. 146.

31 Ibid., p. 150.

32 Ibid., p. 156.

33 Ibid., p. 160.

34 Ibid., p. 168.

35 Ibid., p. 176.

36 Ibid. p. 177.

37 Ibid., p. 180.

38 Carolyn Forché, ed. *Against Forgetting*, (New York: W. W. Norton & Co., 1993), p. 383. Poem used with permission from hit & run press for *Tadeusz Borowski: Selected Poems*, by Tadeusz Borowski, translated by Tadeusz Pioro with Larry Rafferty and Meryl Natchez. Lafayette, CA: hit & run press, 1990.

# If Not Now, When? _____

Primo Levi (New York: Penguin Books), 1986.  ISBN 0-14-0084920-4.

## Glossary

**Einsatzkommandos.** Troops of German officers who conducted mass killings in the villages and ghettos during the Holocaust

**Kaddish.** Jewish prayer for the dead

**L'Khayim.** Traditional Jewish salute: To Life!

**Lager.** Nazi prison camp

**Nivnoye Marshes.** Site of partisan group lead by Venjamin Ivanovich

**Novoselki Camp.** Republic of the Marshes: site of partisan group lead by Dov

**Partisan.** A man or woman not in a regular army who supports guerilla warfare

**Red Army.** Russian Army

**Shokhet.** Person who performs ritual slaughter of kosher (approved) meat

**Trayf.** Non-kosher food; food that is not approved or slaughtered by rabbinical law

**Yeshiva Bucher.** Young, religious, Jewish scholar

## Introduction

### Jewish Resistance to the Nazis

The Jewish resistance movements of Eastern Europe during World War II were organized efforts of bands of Jews and gentiles. Resistance groups were a powerful physical and emotional force. These groups worked together fighting the Nazis, sabotaging the war effort, and freeing and rescuing Jews in the concentration camps of Europe. They viewed their resistance efforts as a means to choose their fate, to take part in their future, and place themselves in history as heroic and courageous survivors.

Unarmed Jewish resistance against the sanctions imposed by the Third Reich began before the start of the war. A political underground that defied Nazi activities was present in the towns and villages of Europe. The formation of the Pioneer Youth Organization encouraged strength and purpose for young Jewish men and women. It gave them a strong sense of community support. Coupled with these groups was the Zionist Youth Organization that prepared communities for immigration to Palestine. Underground presses published and distributed information about the war and Nazi actions. Emissaries traveled the countryside delivering messages to the heads of the Judenrat and Jewish Councils. Members of the resistance movements helped Jews obtain papers for crossing the borders. Resistance activities included the hiding and rescue of Jewish children.

Armed Jewish resistance was organized in three different ways: armed rebellion in the ghettos and death camps, formation of underground partisan groups, and joining of the already established resistance movement in occupied Europe. The most formidable of these groups was the Jewish Fighting Organization in Poland. Comprised of mostly Jewish members, it led groups on sabotage and harassment activities against the Nazis.

Armed rebellions in the ghettos posed a serious threat to the Nazis. The most profound of these rebellions was in the ghetto of Warsaw in April 1943. The Warsaw ghetto was originally comprised of over 500,000 men, women, and children. By the time of the uprising, starvation, disease, and deportations to death camps reduced the population to less than 60,000. Collecting an extremely limited supply of bombs, ammunition, Molotov cocktails, machine guns, and grenades, one thousand resisters held the ghetto for four weeks against more than 3,000 German troops. The ghetto was eventually destroyed, but the news of the courage and fortitude of the resistance fighters bolstered the spirits of Jews in Eastern Europe. Uprisings in the ghettos of Vilna, Bialystok, and Krakow placed the resisters' actions within the pages of the history books.

Revolts in the death camps also took place. In Auschwitz-Birkenau, inmates were able to destroy a crematorium before being sent to their deaths. The men of Sobibor revolted against the German guards with 60 of 600 inmates escaping death.

Those who escaped the death camps, ghettos, and Russian army joined the partisan movements in the woods and marshes of Eastern Europe. These bands of freedom fighters were made up of teenagers, men, and women intent upon choosing their own fate. They stole ammunition, guns, food, and clothing and made their way across Poland attacking the German posts and camps. Cutting telephone wires, intercepting airdrops, rerouting and derailing trains, moving people out of the ghettos, and freeing prisoners in the lagers and camps, these small bands advanced the cause for freedom for the Jews of Europe.

Non-Jewish organizers and individuals also aided in the plight of the Jews. Labeled "The Righteous Few" these men and women risked their lives to save Jews within their communities. Hiding people in barns and attics, taking children into their homes and raising them as their own, ferreting individuals out of the country to safer locations, providing food and clothing to those hiding in the woods, these Righteous Few showed a humanity that was absent in most of Europe.

Rich research work can be done about the resistance movement. Stories, testimonies, and documents can be found and presented in the classroom. For research resources teachers should refer to Suggested Reading in the following analysis of Primo Levi's *If Not Now, When?*

## Character List

Leonid
Mendel
Venjamin
Dov
Gedaleh
Pavel
Ulybin
Piotr
Line
Bella
Sissl
White Rokhele
Black Rokhele
Isidor

### Plot Summary

*If Not Now, When?* is a complex novel set during the final months of World War II. Primo Levi details the experiences of a band of Jewish partisans traveling from Russia through Poland to Italy. Passionate in their roles as subversive agents against the Germans, this band of men, women, and children plan and execute clandestine operations throughout Eastern Europe. The band consists of escapees from the concentration camps and lagers of Europe, survivors of the ghettos, and deserters and lost soldiers from the Russian army. Joined in their political beliefs and dreams of immigrating to Palestine, these courageous people teach us the important lessons of humanity: the significance of community and personal relationships, the power of shared purpose, and the importance of moral and ethical choices.

Primo Levi participated with the Italian partisans during World War II. In writing this novel, he illustrates the determination and courage of a group of men and women who were given the opportunity to persevere in their efforts for freedom. Their resistance movements offered opportunities to fight back, mark their place in history, and defy the power and cruelty of the Nazis. The richness of this fictional piece of literature comes from the detail of the historical and political events of the time. With particular emphasis on the latter years of the war, the strategic settings of World War II unfold in the telling of this story. Teachers may choose to use this novel as a strong historical study of the events of World War II. It includes information on the Russian front, the Allied landing in Italy, and the surrender of Mussolini in Italy.

Living with the terror of the Holocaust, the characters represent qualities and failings of humankind. Through examination of the characters' actions and words, Levi details their personalities and explores the hard philosophical questions about the nature of good and evil. The resisting actions against the Nazis represent more than a voice of protest. For Levi, resistance becomes the declaration of the value of human life. These men, women, and children learn to understand their Jewish identity and relationship with God through their resistance work. Primo Levi uses imaginative language and deep metaphor in his writing to create his characters and their search for meaning in life.

Students should keep a reading journal with notes about the individual characters, settings, and action of the novel. Because there are many questions posed in the telling of this story, students should respond with their reactions and opinions throughout the reading of the book.

### Objectives for Teaching *If Not Now, When?*

In reading *If Not Now, When?* teachers should focus on the historical and political events of the late years of the war and the following ideas:

▶ The role of the partisan groups during the war

▶ The philosophical ideas represented by the characters

▶ The significance of the individual versus the community

This study of *If Not Now, When?* divides the novel into four parts: Part One (Chapters 1, 2, 3) introduces the main characters Mendel and Leonid and their entry into the Novoselki band. Part Two (Chapters 4, 5, 6) brings the band to Ulybin's camp near the village of Turov. Part Three (Chapters 7, 8) follows the band into Poland and Part Four (Chapters 9, 10, 11, 12) takes the troop to Italy. The journey from the ravaged villages of western Russia to the beauty and wonder of Italy is a metaphoric adventure that takes the reader from the depths of despair to action and freedom.

It is important for students to have some background information about Russian involvement in the war. The main characters in this novel are Russian Jews who have served in the Russian army. Their nationalistic pride is evident, but the discrimination and prejudice against Jews in Russia has a strong effect on their position in the war. For centuries, the Jews of Russia suffered under the constraints of the czar and the results of the Russian Revolution placed them in a dangerous and unstable place. Students should research the history of the Jews in Russia and the role Russia played in the eastern front during World War II. (See Suggested Reading.)

### Part One: In the Beginning (Chapters 1, 2, and 3)

"It's almost a year since I spoke with a human being, because it's best for a straggler not to talk."[1]

Writing about his experiences in Auschwitz, Primo Levi commented that it was "the fundamental experience of my life . . . I knew that if I survived, I would have to tell the story."[2] The story that Levi tells in this novel is one of human relationships: the failure and the success of humankind to act morally with each other, the search for God, and the discovery of the importance of community. The exactness and depth in which Levi reveals his characters is the foundation of his writing. Using the resistance movement as the theme, Levi imbues each of his characters and their behavior with bits and pieces of ourselves. The characters symbolize despair, indifference, courage, longing, loss, and hope. Levi masterfully weaves his story of these courageous men and women with the use of internal monologue, dialogue, and description. It is the main character Mendel who becomes the reader's guide in this adventure into the human soul.

The first voice we hear in this novel is Mendel's as he introduces the symbol of the clocks. "Two years before the war began, the bell rope broke . . . so after that he announced the time by shooting a hunting rifle into the air."[3] The bell was the town's source for correct time. The symbol of the broken bell rope replaced by a gun is a powerful metaphor for the approaching war. Civilized measurements of time and human behavior are replaced with the violence of the gun, and when the Nazis come and take the gun away, ". . . the village was left without any time."[4] Thus, human and moral behavior is destroyed in a symbolic gesture. The events of the war exist outside of known time. This opening story introduces us to Mendel, also known as Menachem, the consoler. A twenty-eight-year-old Jewish watchmaker, Mendel is a lost soldier in the Red Army. With the death of his wife in the mass murder in his hometown of Strelka, Mendel wanders the war-torn countryside, hiding from the enemy and the Russian army, searching for peace. His voice becomes the questioning narrator, the observer who tries to understand the confusion and terror of the war. It is important for students to pay close attention to the character Mendel. In his questions and observations, the reader finds the heart of the story: the search for understanding about humanity and God. It is suggested that students keep a "question journal" recording the philosophical dilemmas Mendel discusses with the band of resisters and within himself.

Levi reveals Mendel's nurturing and consoling side through his relationship with Leonid, a young escapee of the German lager. As they begin the early stages of their relationship, Mendel assumes a paternal role with this shy, diffident, and damaged young man. He sees that Leonid "must have something else inside . . . an inner scar, a bruise, perhaps a painful aura around a human face."[5] It is through their dialogue that both characters expose their pasts. Their friendship grows as they seek the common purpose of shelter and peace.

In the early pages of this tale, we hear the voice of Mendel as the philosopher. The questioning begins with Mendel's discussion on the intention of God: ". . . God made the Germans: And why did he make them? Or did he allow Satan to make them? For our sins? And what if man doesn't have any sins? Or a woman?"[6] Mendel becomes the voice that tries to make sense and order of a chaotic world of violence. His questions seek to justify the purposelessness of the Nazis' actions. These fundamental questions of "why" serve as the guide for study of the Holocaust, and students should read carefully for the discoveries Mendel makes along the way to finding answers.

When teachers lead discussions of these questions, they should focus on small-passage analysis; five-sentence paragraph form provides important reading and writing skills. The following are passages spoken by Mendel revealing his understanding and confusion about the world:

▶ "For the Germans, you [Leonid] are an escaped prisoner, in addition to being a Russian and a Jew. For the Russians, you're a deserter, and you're also suspect, you could be a spy." (p. 30)

▶ ". . . when a war's on, everything's different, we have to resign ourselves to being different, too, and maybe it won't do us any harm." (p. 31)

▶ "He no longer felt in his heart the vigor of the young man and soldier, only weariness, emptiness, and a yearning for a white, serene nothingness, like a winter snowfall." (pp. 37–38)

Students should write, then discuss the significant ideas of prejudice, discrimination, and loss represented in these quotes. Teachers can use these questions to develop class discussion and group presentations.

▶ How is a Russian Jew caught in a double bind during the war?

▶ Does the definition of morality change during wartime? How is "difference" a positive and negative aspect of war?

▶ How do Mendel and Leonid continue on their journey despite their "emptiness"? What motivates them to try to discover a community?

Levi surrounds this introspective study with the action and detail of the resistance movement. Moving through their sense of despair together, Leonid and Mendel search for the band of resisters in the Nivnoye marshes on the White Russian border. Map work will reveal where these two men follow the Dnepr River as they approach the border between White Russia and Poland. Description of their two-week journey through the marshes introduces the reader to the life of the wanderer. Mendel is the symbol of the nomadic Jew tortured by his oppressors and searching for his people. As Levi describes the hunger, cold, and wet these men experience, he reveals to the reader the loneliness and endlessness of their quest for community. Students should read carefully the section about the Uzbek pilot as well as the passages about the bartering with the local farmer in order to understand the complexities of trying to stay hidden from the Nazis.

The introduction of the character Venjamin and his band of resisters offers a perspective on a non-Jewish resistance movement. Venjamin wears his Russian army uniform with pride and rules his troop like an army general. There is a certain violence to his demeanor. In Mendel's eyes, Venjamin is "a fearsome human species, a young warrior of prompt and concise movements, intelligent face, and intense but inscrutable gaze."[7] Students should take notes on the leaders of each tribe of resisters to compare the personalities, ways of governing, and goals in their actions of resistance. Careful observation of the difference between the Jewish movement and the Russian band should be noted.

As Leonid and Mendel join the celebration for the Allied landing in Italy, it becomes quickly apparent that this band of resisters will not become their family. Levi uses the men and women of Venjamin's band to explore the anti-Semitism that reigns among the non-Jews of Eastern Europe. With the labeling of Mendel and Leonid by one of the men as "you people" and Venjamin's rejection of Leonid's and Mendel's desire to join the band, Levi emphasizes the prevalent prejudicial stereotypes assigned to Jews. They are dismissed as unlikable and untrustworthy. Venjamin encourages them to find the village of Jewish resisters in Novoselki. This incident of discrimination mirrors the sentiments against Jews in Russia. An interesting supplemental reading for students could be an excerpt from Chaim Potok's *The Fixer*, a novel that details the ethnic prejudices of Russian society. (See Suggested Reading.)

Levi uses his meticulous description in this section of the novel to introduce the methods of sabotage employed by the resisters. Students should read carefully the passages on pages 62–63 in order to understand the mission of the resisters. The following questions should accompany discussion of this event in the novel:

▶ From where do the tree trunks come, and what purpose do they serve for the Germans?
▶ How does Venjamin exercise his authority in this mission?
▶ The destruction of the tree trunks accomplishes both a physical and moral victory for the band. Explain.

Chapter 3 of this book describes the Jewish band of resisters in the fortress of the "republic of the marshes." The old monastery becomes a dream come true for Mendel and Leonid; they are together with Jews who share their past and their dreams for the future. In comparison to Venjamin, the leader Dov represents an alternate type of rule. Dov is the middle-aged man of experience. He rules with a sagacity and thoughtfulness that comes from his keen sensitivities. His story detailed on page 81 provides students insight into the powers of survival. With each man and woman assigned a task, Dov rules with a sense of order in this camp. All work is for the good of each other. The "obsessive, paradoxical order, which each one seemed to maintain with effort and stubbornness, every minute" [8] provides the security and care for which Mendel has been searching. Students should take careful notes on the organization of the camp. The following questions should accompany discussion of these details of the novel:

▶ What sets it apart from Venjamin's troop?
▶ How does Dov maintain his leadership and authority?
▶ What are the rules of the camp?

The entry of Mendel and Leonid into this troop signals the beginning of significant changes in both men. They learn that the first rule of the republic is to leave their stories behind because, "If we kept on telling one another what we've seen, we'd go crazy." [9] This rule gives both men permission to begin to embrace the present and prepare for and anticipate the future. Students should be aware of the subtle changes that begin to take place in these two men. As Leonid separates himself from Mendel in order to establish a relationship with the young girl Line, this allows Mendel to begin to discover his own needs. The relationship between these two men sets Mendel into his philosophical thinking. As Leonid ignores the rule of the camp and endangers his position in the band with his indifference to authority, Mendel questions his role of responsibility to this troubled young man. Reflecting on the biblical story of Cain and Abel, Mendel considers, "Was Leonid his brother? . . . Of course Mendel wasn't his keeper. . . . And yet the itch persisted: Maybe this is how it is, maybe each of us is Cain to some Abel, and slays him in the field without knowing it, through the things he does to him, the things he says to him, and the things he should say to him and doesn't."[10] Revealing his truly compassionate side, Mendel represents the spirit of man that can look beyond his own need for survival in order to care for another human being. Levi uses these two characters to enlarge the questions of the complexities of human relationships and war. It would be interesting for students to read the story of Cain and Abel from Genesis in the Old Testament in order to discuss the issue of responsibility to one's fellow man and woman. Teachers should also see the chapter on Poetry of the Holocaust for a discussion on the poem "Written in Pencil in a Sealed Boxcar."

As students read the detail of sabotaging the railroad, they should be aware of how this mission orchestrated by Dov has a direct effect on Leonid. The derailment of the train becomes not only an act of revenge against the Nazis, but an opportunity for Leonid to find a place for himself in this community, a chance to prove his worth. Dov carefully recognizes Leonid's need to assert himself, and he allows the boy to exercise some authority in order to boost his self-esteem. The following questions should be used to help in the discussion of these crucial passages:

▶ How is the act of sabotage a "present" for Line from Leonid? (p. 88)
▶ How does the limited success of this mission affect Leonid?
▶ Why is the idea of a romance both wonderful and absurd in this time and place?

Historical information about the war is provided in this chapter. Teachers should be careful to note the surrender of Italy, the capturing of Smolensk by the Russians, and the advances of the Allies from the south. Map work is important in this section in order for students to understand the position of the band and the approaching armies. The news from the leader Gedaleh about the "amnesty" for Jews is significant (p. 93). The invitation to return to the ghettos with promises of food and shelter affects the community of resisters. Students should study the use of flyers and propaganda to further the lies and violence of the Nazi Party.

The invitation to the German "hunting party" issued by the legendary leader Gedaleh illustrates the complexity of war. The seemingly "civilized" nature of the hunt turns into a massacre. With German officers shooting at the partisans and the Russians, and the resisters trying to defend themselves with their meager ammunition, Mendel questions their involvement in this mission. As the small band attempts to fight off their attackers, Dov proclaims, "We're fighting for three lines in the history books."[11] It is in this single line that Levi reveals the true mission of the resistance movement. Protesting the accusations that Jews allowed themselves to be slaughtered without resistance, Levi establishes the power and determination of the Jewish people to protest, react, defy, and survive. Levi points out that this story is not being told to detail massacres; he emphasizes the important themes of this novel: it is a story of survival and hope. The troop of resisters journey from their destroyed "republic of the marshes" to join Gedaleh and his band as they seek a new future. Further reading of resistance testimony supports the significant role the men and women of the movement played in the war. (See Suggested Reading.)

## Presentation Ideas

1. Students should create a map of the eastern border of the Soviet Union and Eastern Europe during the war. The route of both the advances of the Soviet army and the resisters should be marked with the significant cities and rivers highlighted. The ghettos of Russia and Poland play a significant role in the resistance movement and should also be marked on the map.

2. The stories of the resistance in the ghettos of Warsaw and Bialystok are mentioned in the first three chapters of the book. Students should be divided into small groups in order to research the testimonies from these two ghettos. Presentations to the class could include film and CD-ROM on the ghetto uprisings. (See Suggested Reading and Videography.)

3. Students should research the life of Primo Levi, his participation in the resistance movement in Italy, and his internment in the death camp Auschwitz-Birkenau. Selections from *Survival in Auschwitz* should be presented to the class as well as Levi's poetry. (See chapter on Poetry of the Holocaust.) The Internet provides interviews and pictures of Primo Levi's home in Italy as well as his return to Auschwitz after the war. (See Internet Sources at the end of the chapter.)

## Writing Ideas

1. The first three chapters of *If Not Now, When?* provide an excellent source for teachers to focus on written and oral character sketches. The following is an outline for the steps of this written and oral project:

   ▶ Students should choose a person in their lives who represent a strong influence on them and write a character study of this individual. Making a list of the physical features of the individual, students should note in detail the eyes, hands, tone of voice, facial expression, and stature of the person. A list can be made of the personality traits of this individual: their demeanor in specific situations, their likes and dislikes, and their opinions and beliefs.

   ▶ Students should then write a paragraph about what they admire most in this person. What do they respect in this individual? What elements of his/her personality do they wish to reflect in themselves?

   ▶ Gathering this preliminary information should then lead to a written character study. This can be done as a straight composition on the person or a narrative telling a story about this person to the reader.

▶Students could also write a monologue in the voice of the person and perform it for the class.

2. The story of *If Not Now, When?* is about a spiritual as well as physical journey that Mendel and the band of resisters take. Students should write a narrative about a "journey" they have taken. Emphasis should be placed on details as to where they "started" and how they "ended" this trip. A journey can be defined as something as simple as crossing the street for the first time alone, sleeping over at a friend's house, traveling to a foreign country, or embarking on a solo sailing adventure. A journey can also be spiritual, as well. Students should be encouraged to "show" their story through storytelling.

3. Leonid and Mendel are searching for community. Students should write their definition of the word community. Where do they find their sense of community? What role does it play in their lives? What are their responsibilities within this community? What is valued in this community? What are the "rules of membership"? Students should read their writing and compare the shared and differing sense of community.

## Part Two: Despair and Renewal (Chapters 4, 5, and 6)

"We're not in Jerusalem yet, but we're out of Babylon."[12]

The middle chapters of this novel give the reader a deeper understanding of the composition of the partisan group and its mission. Levi examines the role of the leader and his relationship with the members of the bands. He also uses these chapters to delve more deeply into the psychological and spiritual journey Mendel and his fellow partisans experience. The political motives of these men are also influenced by their religious beliefs. The reader sees an emerging, stronger sense of the significance of being a Jew and claiming one's religious heritage and traditions.

Study of the camp at Turov and its leaders Ulybin and Gedaleh provides an opportunity for students to discuss and write on the differing methods and ideologies between partisan groups. Ulybin's camp is professionally run with a quartermaster, bunks, linen, mined woods, radio, and a press that circulates propaganda against the Germans. It is comprised mostly of Russians who are not Jewish. The atmosphere of the group is one of determined revenge. Human relationship and comradeship is not part of the design for this camp.

As Mendel begins to find his place within this camp, he has the opportunity to discuss his views and opinions with the character Pavel, a non-Jew, who has loyally aligned himself with this band of resisters. Students should read carefully the discussion between these two men on pages 107–11. As Pavel innocently asks the question, "Why do the Germans want to kill all you people?"[13] he frames the unanswerable questions of all the Jews of Europe. Their discussion about prejudice and difference raises the larger questions of the Holocaust. Pavel understands the inhumanity and evil of the Nazis, yet he struggles with the fact that he must kill in order to prove his worth as a human being. Laced between his words of sympathy for the plight of the Jews are also statements and phrases of discrimination. Students should examine the following quotes for their significant historical prejudice.

▶ "I believe a Russian's worth more than a Chinaman." (p. 110)

▶ "But you're strange people all the same. Strange. . . . And you people always reason too much. Maybe that's why the Germans kill you. . . ." (p. 111)

▶ "But tell me: is it true that it was your people who crucified Jesus?" (p. 113.)

As Pavel tells the story of the yeshiva *bucherim*, the young scholars of God's word, he uses patronizing tones and mockery to capture his audience. His behavior displays the coping mechanisms that Jews of the world were forced to learn in order to survive: laugh first at yourself before you can laugh with others. Students should take careful notes on the character Pavel in order to discuss his growth and commitment to the Jews in their band.

Primo Levi uses the events of sabotage by the partisans to comment on the strength and determination of the members of the band. The men of Ulybin's group are sophisticated in their telephone wiretaps, but when it comes time for Mendel to prove his allegiance to the group, bravado is replaced with true human suffering. Murder does not come easily to this spiritual man and when Ulybin orders him to shoot the Ukrainian, Mendel suffers the inhumanity and terror of his first killing.

Again using the characters Mendel and Leonid as the reader's guide to human emotion, Levi develops the relationship between these two men and the women Line and Sissl. For Leonid, Line becomes his single contact of emotional expression. He withdraws from the remainder of the troop and focuses all his attention on this young girl. He believes she alone will provide the human contact for which he so longs. Line will dispel his isolation and make him whole. Line is a powerful force that acts as a foil to the character Leonid. She represents the strong, unrelenting new Russian Jewish woman, one that has been educated about Western feminist philosophies. She is a woman who sees power as a tool to accomplish her goals. Her intentions are fierce. She will emigrate to Palestine and form a society free of the prejudice and discrimination of Russia. This young woman who sees a future before her is portrayed in sharp contrast to Leonid who has been damaged and nearly destroyed by the events of the war. Through these two characters, Levi examines the devastation and strength that emerges in these survivors.

Mendel also seeks the comfort and joy of human contact in his relationship with Sissl. The passages describing their relationship are poignant in the characterization of their love. It is biblical in its detail. They commune in an "Eden-like" hayloft, innocent in their physical and emotional need for each other. They emerge from the loft renewed as human beings who still have the capacity to love and be loved.

As the reader becomes intimately protective of these characters, Levi catapults them into the dangers of the resistance movement. The mission of intercepting the airdrop from the Nazis serves to emphasize several themes of the book. Ulybin emerges as a commander who works for a purpose with little concern for the human toll war takes upon his band. The risks for the Jews and the Russians in this troop are different, and the outcome of the partisan work will benefit the Russians in more significant ways than the Jews. Mendel considers the complex differences between the Russians and the Jews—a distinction that makes itself most apparent in Ulybin's group. "For the Russians, a longing of home was not an unreasonable hope, even probable: a yearning to go back, a call. For the Jews, the regret for their houses was not a hope but a despair. . . . Their houses no longer existed: they had been swept away, burned by the war or by slaughter, bloodied by the squads of hunters of men. . . . Why go on living, why fight? For what house, what country, what future?"[14] This statement by Mendel captures the despair of the displaced Jews of Russia and Eastern Europe following the war. Teachers should provide information and testimony from the thousands of Jews who were placed in displaced persons camps following the war.

The failure of the airdrop mission illustrates further the discrimination between the Russians and the Jews. Ulybin orders Mendel and several of the younger Jewish boys to mine the barracks—a dangerous and potentially fatal mission. As Mendel protests, Ulybin shouts, "You people are all alike. All good at arguing, and all half German."[15] This tirade brings Mendel to question his position as a Jew. He recognizes himself as the archetypal scapegoat of the Jewish traditions, the one sent up for sacrifice for the sins of the community. Mendel resents this assigned sin placed upon him by Ulybin. He says, "If I've sinned, I bear the burden of my sins. . . . I don't bear the sins of anybody else."[16] Mendel refuses to be the scapegoat for Ulybin and is determined to continue on without bearing the responsibility of the leader's actions.

Gedaleh provides the humanity of leadership for which Mendel is searching. The alliance with this leader takes this small group of men and women on not only a physical journey, but a spiritual one as well. Gedaleh is the leader of mythic proportions. His personal escape from the concentration camps and his allegiance to the resistance movement make him a powerful leader. A soulful violinist, he brings to these survivors of the pogroms, ghettos, and mass-killing sites a compassionate and sensitive voice. His violin playing speaks of the sorrow of the past and the hope of the future. He is the Pied Piper of the Holocaust who will save these people who are "tired, poor, and dirty, but not defeated."[17] Although Ulybin's group resents Gedaleh, they recognize the strength of this band. Supported by headquarters in Russia, this group of resisters holds a certain power that exceeds Ulybin's reign. Students should read the passages on pages 150–51 for a full understanding of Gedaleh and his followers. Using the descriptors "lighthearted," "intoxicated with their new freedom," "fierce," "vengeance," and "victorious," Levi paints a picture of a humanity that survives "because they had seen the superman struggling in the icy water like the frogs: a present no one could take from them."[18] Their triumphs over the Germans give them a purpose to continue in their quest for freedom.

Gedaleh becomes for Mendel his spiritual guide, a man with whom he talks about his heritage and spirituality. His references to the Torah, the Five Books of Moses, are the guide to answering many of Mendel's questions of faith. On page 161, Gedaleh tells Mendel that Jews have weak memories, but they remember one thing: the defeat of Amalek. The story of Amalek would be an interesting one for students to read. The biblical reference can be found in the book of Exodus, chapter 17, lines 8 through 16. Amalek represents a powerful symbol for the Jewish people. As the Jews emerge from captivity in Egypt and begin their wanderings in the desert, they complain to their leader Moses about their lack of water, food, and shelter. In a weakened state, they question the ways of this God who is leading them to the Promised Land, asking the question, "Why did you bring us out of Egypt, to kill us and our children and livestock with thirst?"[19] God strengthens these people, and they fight to defeat the Amalekites, a tribe determined to eradicate the Jews. God vows to blot out the memory of Amalek and lead the Jewish people to the Promised Land.

The tribe of Amalek historically becomes the symbol of evil for the Jews. In the Book of Esther, the evil Haman, a descendant of the tribe of Amalek, pledges to kill all the Jews. Again, God supports his people against this attack, and they fight the Romans. Like the Jews of the Bible, Mendel questions the God of the Jews: "Why are we being punished? For what sins?" Gedeleh responds by referring to the Nazis and their leader Hitler as the modern Amalek. He repeats God's pledge to "extinguish even the memory of Amalek"[20] through the actions of the resistance movement. Gedaleh gives hope and promise to Mendel in his spiritual faith in God. He makes meaningful the band's struggle to live and defeat their enemies. The call for the destruction of the memory of Amalek resounds in the call of the Holocaust to never forget the plight of the millions who died in their battle against Hitler, the modern Amalek.

And so the resistance becomes the battle cry for the Jews of the present and the past. Levi describes this movement with all the characteristics of a true group of soldiers. They have anthems, poetry, and songs that lead them in their pursuit for justice. Levi's experience in the resistance movement made him familiar with the music and poetry that lead these brave men and women. Students should examine the song on page 168 sung by Gedaleh. This "anthem," with its marching rhythms, is a call for victory. The song makes reference to the historical suffering of the Jews who "Withered in the shadow of the cross" (l. 4) of the Christian believers. The poem rallies the people with its pride in their resistance actions at the prison camps Sobibor and Treblinka. And the words of Hillel "If not for myself, who will be for me? /If not this way, how? If not now, when?" (l. 7–8) resound for Mendel and the resistance fighters. Reading the story of Hillel would help students understand the commitment Jews make to retain their beliefs in the face of unrelenting evil and attack. Rabbi Hillel lived in the first century before the Common Era. Hillel represents the model for just and ethical human behavior. His commitment to study and faith in God led his fellow scholars in the pursuit of moral behavior.[21] Many of his teachings can be found in the text of the Jewish tract *Pirkei Avot, Ethics of the Fathers*. This book discusses the righteousness of humankind and its responsibility to justice and fairness. (See Presentation Ideas for further instruction topics.)

Gedaleh's teachings of Hillel lead to the story of Martin Fontasch. Teachers should refer to the chapter on Poetry of the Holocaust for the poem "Shema" by Primo Levi for a more complex understanding of this story.

The spiritual journey becomes an adventure as Gedaleh leads his troop onto the train into Poland. Gedaleh asks for God's blessing as they enter the "inhabited world."[22]

## Presentation Ideas

1. The character Line is presented as a strong feminist who expresses her understanding of the future of women in the modern world. Students should research the changing role of women before and during World War II. Some suggested topics are:
   - ▶ The suffragette movement in the United States and England
   - ▶ The "Rosie the Riveter" syndrome in the United States and women's roles in the armed forces
   - ▶ Emma Goldman and her influence on the Communist Party in the United States

2. Gedaleh's band of men and women see their future in emigrating to the land of Palestine. Students should research the historical and political position of Palestine before and during the war. The following are questions that can be used to begin research:
   - ▶ What is the biblical promise to the Jews of the Promised Land? What is God's covenant with Abraham that establishes the Jewish state?
   - ▶ What was the British involvement in Palestine? What were the borders of the land? Who were the primary residents? What was the political system established there?
   - ▶ What was the political policy of Britain in regard to the immigration of Jews from Europe? What difficulties did the Jews face against Great Britain? Against the resident population?
   - ▶ What was the result of the conflict between the resident population, the British army, and the Jews? How was it achieved?

3. As the Allies pushed toward the German lines, the Nazis began dismantling the death camps and the lagers. Students should read personal testimonies detailing the breakup of the camps and the movement of thousands of prisoners across Poland and Germany. Presentations should be made to the class with maps detailing the geographical locations of the camps and the routes of the forced marches. Students could read excerpts from Eli Wiesel's *Night* detailing the forced marches. (See chapter on *Night*.)

**Writing Ideas**

1. The characters Mendel, Gedaleh, and Line become more defined in these middle chapters. Students should choose one character to focus on and make a list of the personality traits. The following questions should guide them in their research:

   ▶ What is the personal history of these characters? What hardships have they endured? What lasting impressions has war made upon them?

   ▶ What are the strengths and weaknesses of the character's personality?

   ▶ How do these affect the character's role in the resistance movement?

   ▶ What does the character think he/she must do in order to survive? What does the character need in order to survive?

   After gathering and noting this information about the character, students should write a monologue or journal entry in the voice of the character. Incorporating the answers to these questions and making reference to the actual events of the story, students should focus on capturing the spirit and beliefs of their character. Oral presentations should be made to the class.

2. Hillel's commentaries on the Five Books of Moses became proverbs to study and live by for the Jewish people. Students should collaborate to write their own *Ethics of the Fathers and Mothers*. What lessons would they pass down to the next generation? This collection of proverbs could be made into an illustrated chapbook, including poetry and personal essays. It could be printed for exhibition in the school's library.

3. Choosing Dov, Ulybin, or Gedaleh, students should make an artistic shield that represents the mission of the band of resisters. Inscribed on the shield should be an insignia and motto that best represent the sentiment and mission of the troop.

## Part Three: A New Direction (Chapters 7 and 8)

"We're not orphans any more, and we're not stray dogs any more."[23]

Chapters 7 and 8 of this novel take us into the interior of Poland and the hearts of Mendel and Leonid. With their movement into Poland and the re-acquaintance with the world outside of the partisan camps, these two characters give themselves permission to feel human emotion and need beyond hunger and fear. The relationship described between Line and Leonid and then Mendel is a poignant portrayal of the awakening of passion and physical comfort. The philosophical questions of the war become more personal and introspective. For Mendel and Leonid, the choices are about moral behavior and friendship. Students should read pages 192–95 to gain an understanding of these changes in the characters. Teachers can use these quotes to develop class discussion.

   ▶ "Mendel felt desire invade him . . . the desire [to be] . . . away from the roads, weapons, fears, and memories of the slaughter." (pp. 191–92)

   ▶ "Rivke, please go away. Go back to where you came from, let me live." (p. 192)

▶ "I am the woman of no one, and by resisting you, I bind you to me." (p. 193)

▶ "If you haven't killed him yourself, [you] who were his brother, and when they asked you to account for him, you answered with the insolence of Cain?" (p. 195)

The taking of the lager is one of the most moving and complicated sections of this novel. The story of Leonid's death is filled with terror and questions. Mendel recognizes that the young boy Leonid is damaged by the events of the war. Returning to the metaphor of the broken watch, "Mendel remembers that he had once compared Leonid to a watch clogged with dust . . . the springs had become tangled, they ran a bit slow, then they were wildly fast for a bit, and all of them in the end were broken beyond repair." Leonid then becomes the symbol of the Jew who is unable to rise above and beyond the experiences and horrors of the Holocaust, yet another innocent victim of the evil of the Nazis.

The goal of the mission is multifaceted. The partisans are determined to free any remaining prisoners and kill the Germans who guard the area. But this mission also becomes an emotional journey for every member of the troop. For some, this is their first encounter with the barbed wire, the stench of burning flesh, and the broken bodies of the prisoners. For others, this camp serves as a reminder of their past, the fate of their families who died in the camps, and the empty future. The battle for recognition and self-worth still rages within Leonid, and he uses the lager event in a fatal attempt to prove himself. The questions that surround Leonid's death are often difficult for students to grasp. What did his leap into the rounds of gunfire mean? Was this an act of bravery or suicide?

As the group mourns the death of this young man, they also debate Gedaleh's motives in appointing Leonid the leader of the mission. The debate on pages 229–30 shows the fear, determination, sorrow, and steely purpose of the members of this group. Perhaps Line's evaluation of their leader is the most accurate: "Gedaleh has many faces. . . . That's why it's hard to understand him. . . . He flings everything behind him. Today's Gedaleh flings yesterday's Gedaleh behind him." [24] Line understands that it is this endurance that is leading the troop out of Poland to their freedom. As Mottle inscribes the Hebrew letters "V'nosnu, and they will pay back," [25] on the wall of the lager, he emphasizes the presence of retribution in this war and the power of the will to survive.

These chapters also serve to give important historical information about the partisan movement and the war. Levi introduces the role of the partisan group the Jewish Combat Organization and the NSZ, the National Armed Forces of Poland. The history of anti-Semitism in Poland is mentioned as Gedaleh negotiates with the Polish soldiers who resent the presence of a Jewish troop of partisans. Students should consider what the different goals of these two groups are. How do the goals of Gedaleh's group oppose the dreams of the Poles? What advantages does a Jewish group of partisans provide for Poland? Levi also gives factual information in his accounts of the Allied forces landing in Normandy and their advance on Paris. Included in this historical information, the news of the dismantling of the concentration camps is revealed. The events of the unsuccessful attempt to assassinate Hitler and the Warsaw ghetto uprising serve to uplift the spirit of the group (pp. 216–17). These historical facts are an important tool for use in the classroom to further the understanding of the events of the war and explain the fervency of the partisan groups. (See Presentation Ideas for classroom project suggestions.)

## Presentation Ideas

1. Chapters 7 and 8 are rich in their historical data of the war. Dividing the students into small groups, teachers should use the following as the themes for further research:
   - ▶ Warsaw ghetto uprising
   - ▶ Allied landings in Normandy and the advance of the Allied western front
   - ▶ Nazi dismantling of the concentration and death camps and the forced marches
   - ▶ Liberation of the camps by partisan groups and allied soldiers

   There are multiple sources for research in this project. Personal testimony, film footage, and Internet sites provide valuable information. Students could also be divided into teams focusing on presentation method with students working on audio-visual tools, artistic representations, map work, and posters.

## Writing and Visual Art Ideas

1. These two chapters provide a rich opportunity for creative writing. The following are writing prompts for journal work or more formal assignments:
   - ▶ Write journal entries in the voices of the characters Mendel, Sissl, Leonid, and Line in response to the emotional involvement between these couples.
   - ▶ The reader hears very little from Mendel after the taking of the lager. Write a diary entry in his voice expressing his most inner thoughts about this sorrowful event.
2. Write a narrative essay or poem about your most courageous moment. Remember that courage is defined not only by physical bravery, but by emotional fortitude.
3. Create a monument for the lager at Chmielnik. Consider the lives of the prisoners and the partisans that were lost in this camp. Your artwork should include an inscription to those innocent men and women who died in the camp.
4. Draw a portrait of one of the main characters. Consider the detail provided by Levi of their physical and emotional features.
5. Time is a recurring symbol in this novel. Write a poem or create a sculpture or drawing that represents your personal definition of time.

## Part Four: Next Year in Jerusalem (Chapters 9, 10, 11, and 12)

> Bells: yes, those were bells, a faint tolling, delicate, filtered through the earth that buried them; a toy music box playing festively, and it meant that the war was over.[26]

Primo Levi begins the final months of this moving tale during the spring of 1944. With this symbol of rebirth, the author leads the reader out of the trenches of the hiding partisans into the war-torn towns and villages of Poland and Germany. As they continue to sabotage and undermine the Nazi efforts, Gedaleh and his band of courageous men and women expectantly move toward their unknown future. Levi gives the reader a solid background of the events of the war at this time in the novel. The war has been raging for five years. Warsaw is destroyed, and the Russian Army is advancing methodically across Eastern Europe, and the Polish partisans are still fighting. It is under these circumstances that Gedaleh and his troop make their way toward Italy with the rumored promise of illegal ships leaving for Palestine.

The political and emotional conflicts that emerge during this part of their journey are complex. Students should take careful notes on the new set of characters that is introduced in these chapters. The members of the Polish Internal Army represent the continued partisan efforts of the Poles and the resentment toward the Jews of Poland. The conversations with these partisans reveal the differences in their missions. The Polish partisans are fighting to regain their lands, establish a Polish government, and reclaim their homes and positions in their communities. They have a place that represents home while the Jews of Eastern Europe are without that privilege. Yet their leader Edek understands the precarious hope of a free Poland: "The Russians will drive the Nazis out of our country . . . but then they won't go away."[27] Teachers should provide supplemental material explaining the advance of the Russians in the occupied territories. These military positions become the foundation for the eventual takeover of the eastern block in Europe by the Russians.

Within these important pages of the novel, Primo Levi finally gives the reader the full story of Gedaleh's past. His tale of terror and struggle is the archetype of the Jewish experience during the Holocaust. The details of his experiences in the Bialystok ghetto, his hiding with the nuns, and the eventual joining with the rebels against the Nazis are a map of the experiences of thousands of Jews. Gedaleh's dream of the "Promised Land" for the Jews represents a homeland where Jews will no longer be outsiders, a country where they are free to practice their religious beliefs without prejudice and terror. (See Presentation Ideas for further instructional topics.)

These late chapters give the reader graphic details of the partisan work against the Nazis. The battle against the German artillery describes the terror and violence of the partisan work. Students should read these sections carefully for an understanding of the physical and emotional damage of these actions. The philosophic questions that are posed by the group represent the very fiber of discussion about the ethics of war. Mendel is shattered by the deaths of the men from his troop as well as the Nazis. His questions about murder and retribution are difficult ones without answers. Students should give particular attention to pages 250–54 in order to understand the debate and confusion within Mendel. The ethical justification of war versus the inhumanity of man against man is the foundation of discussion for this novel.

Levi takes the reader through a series of events characterizing the tumultuous journey toward Italy. The following are detailed sections of the novel that students should study for their representative ideas of hope, despair, and promise:

Each of these episodes embodies within its story the heightened emotion of the troop as it attempts to recognize its dream of freedom. As new bonds form between the members of Gedaleh's band, Levi creates the hope of the future. The men and women allow themselves to love and form unions as human emotions replace the despair and hopelessness of their past lives. The symbol of hope is represented by the marriage of White Rokhele and Isidor, and her pregnancy gives the promise of a new generation of Jews.

Levi returns to the symbol of the bells and time as a signal for change. Dov leaves the band to rejoin the Russian army and White and Black Rokhele, Mendel, Pavel, Piotr, Sissl, Line, Bella, and Gedaleh are all that remain of the partisan group. Traveling now like a small family, these men and women slowly move themselves through the ruins of Germany. While detained by the Russians in Golgau, the troop temporarily loses its purpose and direction. Deprived of its freedom to move on, helpless without ammunition, the group struggles to redefine its identity. Questions arise about who they are and what they represent without family and partisan work. The movement toward their dream becomes ephemeral. Students should read carefully for the political and social implications facing the Jews when the Russians incarcerate the band. Torn between its allegiances to their homeland of Russia and commitments to its position in the Russian army, the group must choose between loyalty to a cause or themselves. The character Captain Smirnov represents the conflict—he is Jewish and a Russian patriot who chooses to stay with his homeland allegiances. The dialogue between Smirnov and the partisans characterizes the conflict of emotions and political allegiances.

The group chooses to continue its journey toward Italy. Levi paints a horrifying landscape of the towns and villages of Germany. Moving through the towns of Neuhaus and Dresden, they encounter the hostility and fear of the remaining Germans. The human column of refugees reminds them of their lost families, and the anti-Semitism of the country is recognizable in the faces of the people of the towns. The death of Black Rokhele signals the return of terror and hatred. Seeking revenge and retribution, the attack on the Germans is less a partisan action than a moment of sheer rage and violence. Students should take note of the questions that now plague Mendel. Exhausted by the hatred, despairing at the loss of lives, hopeless in his thoughts of an eventual peace, Mendel declares, "Blood isn't paid for with blood. Blood is paid for with justice."[28] It is this very human anguish that signals the turning point for the troop. As the train takes them into the hills of Italy, this incident seals their involvement in the partisan movement and moves them forward in their pursuit of a new life.

The visual depiction of the view from the doors of the train symbolizes a new beginning. Levi paints a picture of "fertile fields . . . lakes and woods"[29] that stimulates the senses and renews the spirit. The marshes and the pits of Russia fade in the distance as the civilized world emerges for Gedaleh and his people.

Donning civilian clothes in a symbolic act of shedding their former identities, these exhausted men and women become children delighted at the luxury of a pair of stockings, a white blouse, a toothbrush, and a bar of soap. As students read these pages for the description of the "real world" they should consider the following questions:

▶How does the stealing of the truck illustrate both the innocence and power of these men and women?

▶What are the preparations for re-entry? What is comforting and familiar? What is new and unknown?

▶What do the letters DP signify? How does this classification affect the group's future?

▶How does Gedaleh's version of Hillel's proverb, "If not this way, how? If not now, when?" change in tone and interpretation?[30]

The move into Italy also brings a new vocabulary to the band. Hearing for the first time of the gas of the death camps, they are apprised of a new reality. Amazed by the civility of Italy's treatment of the Jews during the war, facing a world without pogroms or prejudice, the men and women must gradually adjust to this awkward feeling of safety. Students should examine the details of the party at the home of Signora Adele S for its emotional implications. Mendel feels ". . . disoriented in a living room filled with beautiful things and polite people; and he felt also like a pawn in a gigantic cruel game."[31] His disorientation characterizes the difficulty of Holocaust survivors after the war. As East European survivors, their experiences differ greatly from the stories of the Italian men and women involved in the crush of the war. After the war, the Italians can claim their homeland and heritage, their privilege of wealth and education, their rights to free government. Mendel and his "family" of partisans look to a new beginning because of need, not choice.

The birth of Isidor and Rokhele's baby boy is the sustainable dream of a new future for these men and women. As Mendel gazes at Line, he pledges himself to all his memories of Line, his wife Rivke, his lost family. He is ready to start a new life. With the news of the bombing of Hiroshima, this band of survivors faces a new and unpredictable future—one that they embrace with joy and promise.

**Presentation Ideas**

1. The movement of Gedaleh's group across Eastern Europe provides students rich opportunities for map work. Students should be divided into small groups and assigned regions of the map. Important battles and the towns and cities should be marked on the map along with the path the partisans take. Students should research the advance of the Russian army and the Allies in order to understand the strategic locations of warfare. Groups can also find personal testimonies from survivors and soldiers to support the research.

2. The battle of Dresden is mentioned in this novel as well as the destruction of key cities in Europe. A supplemental reading selection from Kurt Vonnegut's

*Slaughterhouse Five* or *The Children's Crusade: A Duty Dance with Death* would provide interesting information about the destruction of Dresden. To accompany this study, teachers could prepare a unit on the anti-war movement of World War II.

3. The term DP, Displaced Person, is assigned to the scores of survivors who had no homes to which they could return after the war. Students could research the following questions for a greater understanding of the fate of the Displaced Persons:

   ▶Who organized the Displaced Persons' camps?

   ▶Where were they located?

   ▶Who was eligible for aid in these camps? What aid was provided?

   ▶What part did the Jewish relief agencies in the United States play in the relocation of these people?

4. Levi closes his book before the partisans embark upon their journey to the land of Palestine. The novel *Exodus*, by Leon Uris, and the film adaptation of this story are important tools in teaching the next stage of life for Holocaust survivors. Students should read selections from the book before viewing the movie in order to understand the political unrest of the resettling of this region of the world.

5. The play *The Wall*, by John Hersey, describes the building of the wall around the Warsaw ghetto. Students could do an in-class reading of this piece of literature that characterizes the destruction of the Warsaw ghetto.

## Writing Ideas

1. Into the final chapters of this novel, Levi weaves the symbol of spring as rebirth and new hope. Drawing on their personal memories and associations with spring, students should write poetry that reflects this representative image.

2. Gedaleh's group is grateful for the smallest necessities and luxuries of life. Students should pledge to give up one "necessity" in their lives for one week, keeping a journal that records the implications of this "sacrifice." In choosing this necessity, students should be careful to define what is "necessary" to sustain the quality of their everyday life. Some suggestions for the students could be: driving a car, electricity after dark, showers, purchasing any material goods, the use of the telephone, visiting with friends after school, using a computer.

3. Students could write an epilogue for this novel portraying the characters ten years after the war. Using background information from the book, the epilogue should describe the emotional and physical journey these men and women might make after the end of the war.

## Suggested Reading

Bauer, Yehuda. *Flight and Rescue: The Organized Escape of the Jewish Survivors of Eastern Europe, 1944-48*. New York: Random House, 1970.

Czerniakow, Adam. *The Warsaw Diary of Adam Czerniakow*. New York: Stein and Day, 1979.

**Books**

Gutman, Yisrael and Asrael Gutman. *The Warsaw Ghetto Uprising*. New York: Houghton Mifflin Co., reprint edition, 1998.

Laska, Vera. *Women in the Resistance and in the Holocaust*. Westport, Connecticut: Greenwood Publishing Group, 1983.

Levin, Nora. *The Holocaust Years: The Nazi Destruction of European Jewry, 1933–1945*. Florida: Friege Publishing Company, Inc., 1990.

Poliakov, Leon. *Harvest of Hate: The Nazi Program for the Destruction of the Jews in Europe*. New York: Holocaust Library, 1978.

_____. *The History of Anti-Semitism, Vols. I and II*. New York: Vanguard Press, 1965.

Rashke, Richard. *Escape from Sobibor*. Chicago and Urbana: University of Illinois Press, 1995.

Scholl, Inge. *Students Against Tyranny: The Resistance of the White Rose, Munich, 1942–1943*. Middletown, CT., Wesleyan University Press, 1983.

Schulman, Faye. *A Partisan's Memoir: Women of the Holocaust*. Toronto, Canada: Second Story Press, 1995.

Suhl, Yuri. *They Fought Back. The Story of Jewish Resistance in Nazi Europe*. New York: Crown Publishing, 1967; Schocken Books, 1975.

Tec, Nechama. *The Bielski Partisans*. New York: Oxford University Press, 1994.

Zipperstein, Steven J. *Imagining Russian Jewry: Memory, History, Identity*. Seattle, Washington: University of Washington Press, 1999.

**See Bibliography for Additional Fictional Selections**

Malamud, Benard. *The Fixer*. Penguin USA Reissue, 1994.

Uris, Leon. *Exodus*. Bantam Books Paperback Reissue, 1983.

_____. *Mila 18*. Bantam Books Paperback Reissue, 1983.

**Videography**

*Daring to Resist: Three Women Face the Holocaust*. Women Make Movies. Martha Lubell Productions.

*David*. Social Studies School Services

*Escape from Sobibor*, Social Studies School Services

*The Bielski Brothers: The Unknown Partisans*, Social Studies School Services

*The Courage to Care.* Anti-Defamation League of B'nai B'rith

*The Warsaw Ghetto.* Social Studies School Services

*The Partisans of Vilna.* YIVO Institute for Jewish Research

*The White Rose.* Social Studies School Services

## Internet Sources

http://www.giotto.org/piccolomini/levi.html

http://www.remember.org/guide/wit.root.wit.res.html

Books

[1] Primo Levi, *If Not Now, When?* (New York: Penguin Books, 1986), p. 28.

[2] Ibid.

[3] Ibid., p. 19.

[4] Ibid.

[5] Ibid., p. 46.

[6] Ibid., p. 28.

[7] Ibid., p. 60.

[8] Ibid., p. 81.

[9] Ibid., p. 74.

[10] Ibid., pp. 83–84.

[11] Ibid., p. 98.

[12] Ibid., p. 163.

[13] Ibid., p. 109.

[14] Ibid., p. 136.

[15] Ibid., p. 146.

[16] Ibid.

[17] Ibid., p. 149.

[18] Ibid., pp. 150–51.

[19] *Tanakh: The Holy Scriptures* (New York: The Jewish Publication Society, 1988), p. 111.

[20] Levi, p. 161.

[21] Rabbi Joseph Telushkin, *Jewish Literacy: The Most Important Things You Should Know About the Jewish Religion, Its People, and Its History* (New York: William Morrow and Co., Inc., 1991), p. 122.

[22] Levi., p. 179.

[23] Ibid., p. 181.

[24] Ibid., p. 229.

[25] Ibid., p. 226.

[26] Ibid., p. 270.

[27] Ibid., p. 243.

[28] Ibid., p. 305.

[29] Ibid., p. 315.

[30] Ibid., p. 286.

[31] Ibid., p. 341.

# The Shawl and Rosa

Cynthia Ozick (New York: Vintage International), 1980. ISBN 0-679-72926-7.

**Books**

## Glossary

**Analogy.** A comparison of two or more things of similar characteristics

**Incarceration:** To be enclosed or restricted

**Metaphor.** A single word or phrase in which a name or a quality is attributed to something which is not directly applicable; example: nerves of steel

**Metaphysical.** Concerned with the ultimate of abstract thought and feeling

**Minimalist.** A writer who reduces language to the smallest possible degree

**Neurological.** Pertaining to the system of the nerves

**Phylogeny (Phylogenic).** A history of the development of a species or group of related organisms

**Repressed.** Thoughts, ideas, and feelings kept down, suppressed

**Symbol.** Something used to represent an idea, emotion, or event

## Character List

Rosa
Stella
Magda
Mr. Persky
James W. Tree, Ph.D.

### Plot Summary

*The Shawl* and *Rosa*, by Cynthia Ozick, are a short story and novella written seven years apart. The first story details the brutality of the concentration camps during World War II. Rosa enfolds her baby Magda in a shawl in an effort to protect her from the horror of concentration camp life. Rosa's fourteen-year-old niece, Stella, takes the shawl away from Magda for her own comfort. In a desperate search for the shawl and attempt to save her baby, Rosa witnesses the brutal murder of her child at the hands of a German soldier.

In the sequel novella *Rosa*, Rosa has moved to Miami, Florida, after destroying her used-furniture shop in New York. In an interior monologue, the reader learns of the desperate and lonely life of this woman who struggles between the real relationship with Stella and her fantastical life with the dead Magda.

### Objectives for Teaching *The Shawl* and *Rosa*

In examining these two connected stories, the teacher should focus on the following ideas:

▶The creation and use of metaphor/analogy in depicting a Holocaust story
▶Examination of the life of a Holocaust victim: before, during and after
▶Imagination and reality
▶Philosophies that control lives: Buddhism and Rosa's philosophy on life and death

### Part One: The Use of Metaphor

> [Ms. Ozick] had a great and abiding fear of . . . making art out of the Holocaust, of 'mythopoeticising,' making little stories out of a torrent of truth. [1]

The study of *The Shawl* allows students to engage in an intense examination of the use of metaphor to create the story. Unlike the personal testimony of many survivors that depends on accurate observation, the story uses analogy to create the images of the characters' experiences and inner thoughts. The metaphoric writing of Ozick uses language and sentence styling to enhance the ideas of the story. Accurate depiction of detail is supported by color, taste, smell, touch, and sound in imagery evoking profound feeling and analogous meaning between the two stories.

Focus ideas of metaphor:
▶The shawl (life, death, obsession, renewal)
▶Description of Magda
▶Description of Stella
▶The physical setting

The physicality of the shawl becomes a character in itself as Ozick develops it to enfold, strangle, and join together the three characters' lives. As the story develops, the shawl changes in its representative imagery. It emerges as a maternal protector for Magda who is "a squirrel in its nest, safe, no one could reach inside the little house of the shawl's winding." [2] The entire first chapter redefines over and over the dimensions of the metaphoric piece of fabric; it is the mother that Rosa cannot be. It provides sustenance to a starving baby, warmth, comforting rhythm during a walk, and a safe place to hide from the Germans during the days in the camp. Students should look carefully at the section on pages 6–8 that defines the baby and her dependence on the shawl.

The shawl also turns into a symbol of the terror and brutality inmates were forced to experience in the camps. For Stella, the shawl is a coveted item, a representation for all she misses with great longing. While the fabric comforts the baby Magda, Stella, a child herself, becomes a "cannibal" and harbinger of jealousy and despair. The shawl evolves into Jacob's coat of many colors, a source of hate and despair for Stella. It becomes the death shroud for Magda when ". . . Stella took the shawl away and made Magda die."[3]

The shawl also depicts the loss of individual voice in the camps. Students should read the section on voice on page 7 making note of the metaphoric qualities of Magda's silence. Stuffed inside Magda's mouth, the shawl acts to deprive this child of identity through voice, as it also silences her for her own protection. When deprived of her shawl, the voice of this child emerges as a heartrending wail that is the first sound from her throat. Ozick uses the sound as a metaphoric symbol: the cry for "Ma . . . aaa" is both a cry for the shawl and Rosa. The power of voice is emphasized in the sound of the dead inmates urging Rosa to save her baby with the shawl. These voices urge, instruct, and defy the command of the German soldier, to no avail. As Rosa witnesses the murder of her child, she silences her suffering, deeply burying it inside her. ". . . and Rosa drank Magda's shawl until it dried."[4]

Ozick uses simile and metaphor to create the images of her characters. The accurate, observant nature of the writing is replaced with a swirl of language that develops the nature of the characters. Students should pay close attention to the physical description of Magda stressing the color of her hair, the shape of her body, the look in her eyes, and the movement toward her death. Her physical presence is the embodiment of all who suffered at the hands of the Germans: frail, starving, and desperate. Ozick also gives hints to her paternal roots with the description of the blue eyes and yellow hair.

Physical setting is also a metaphoric tool for Ozick. Students need to read carefully the description of the camp with its detailed accounts of the wind, the barrenness of the landscape inside the camp, and the meadows beyond the fence. This setting is later developed as an analogous symbol in the novella *Rosa*.

Although Ozick is concerned with the use of metaphor to relate the details of the Holocaust, *The Shawl* emerges as a critical piece of literature because of its use of language and style. There is no melodramatic voice, but rather a sincere and profound use of rhythm to relate the events of the story. Students should look carefully at the following sections to study the incantatory nature of this writing. The use of periodic sentences mixed with long, detailed passages creates both the urgency and profundity of intent:

- ▶The introductory paragraph (p. 3)
- ▶Magda's walk across the courtyard in search of the shawl (p. 7)
- ▶The "voices" (p. 9)
- ▶The final paragraph (p. 10)

## Part Two: Parallel Development of Metaphor in Rosa

She saw everything, but as out of invention, out of imagination. . . .[5]

The significant presence of the shawl in the first story gains even more importance by its physical absence in Rosa's life in the novella *Rosa*. All the maternal characteristics of the shawl in the camp are missing. Rosa's life is absent of the representative images of the shawl: love, comfort, and physical and emotional touch. Indeed, Ozick describes her as a "madwoman, and a scavenger."[6] The sparseness of her life with its meager portions of food, human contact, and emotional warmth offer an oppositional view to the nourishment the shawl provides in the first story.

The image of the shawl then becomes the focus of Rosa's fantastical obsession. Teachers should focus on the metaphoric qualities that the shawl possesses for Rosa:

▶ Ritualistic behavior that Rosa creates in her preparation for the opening of the package (p. 45)
▶ Incantatory nature of summoning Magda through the shawl

Students should look closely at the incident of the lost underpants as the object of obsession replacing the shawl. Rosa counts the items of laundry to create a list that gives dimension to her existence. The underpants represent more than a physical loss, but act as a symbol for the loss of the shawl, too. The use of language is particularly effective in this section and students should make note of how Ozick defines this loss and its parallel significance to the shawl. Words like "thieves, stranger, empty, degrading, embarrassed, stains, sexual habits"[7] act as images that defy the sacred nature of the other lost object and defile the memory and power of the shawl. Where the shawl sustains the fantasy of Magda's life, the underpants cement the reality of the present life.

As Rosa must confront the world that surrounds her and choose between self-exile and assimilation into the real world, the power of the shawl diminishes. That which has sustained her fades at her summons; as reality replaces fantasy, Rosa realizes that "the drudgery of reminiscence brought fatigue, she felt glazed and lethargic."[8] Students should keep in their journals the events that transform Rosa, focusing on the following:

▶ The meeting of Persky
▶ Receiving the package from Stella
▶ The ritual of daily activities versus the ritual of the shawl
▶ The phone call to Stella

The themes of the real and imaginary worlds of Rosa's mind are best developed through the letters Rosa receives and composes. Examining the letters carefully, students will be able to define both the characters and their representative images. The character Stella retains her image in Rosa's mind as the source of all evil. With description synonymous with the devil on earth, Stella is labeled as a "cannibal." Rosa describes her as "cold" and the "Angel of Death."[9] Stella becomes the object of anger and resentment for Rosa's sorrow over the loss of her daughter. Although Rosa does remember Stella as a beautiful child, she transforms the girl into a "bloodsucker." Stella represents the real world of loss and sorrow, both past and present. As Stella writes of her own difficulties surviving in the world of New York, what could be shared sentiments and memories between them only serve as a chafing reminder of who they were and who they are. Stella embodies both the reality and the imagination of Rosa.

The letters become crucial in Ozick's use of metaphor to create the character Magda. Through this correspondence with the dead child, Rosa creates and redefines the child grown into a woman. Here reality completely disappears in the obsessional qualities of Rosa's fantasy. Looking carefully at the metaphor of the imagined Magda, students should consider the following questions:

▶How does the letter to Magda illuminate the historical past? (pp. 40–41)

▶What does she represent to Rosa in her barren state of existence?

▶How is Magda's "growth" representative of both hers and Rosa's lost potential?

▶Where do reality and fantasy clash for Rosa, and why?

Just as the letters to Magda emphasize the fantasy of Rosa's life, the letters from Dr. Tree pull her into the real world. His letters cause a paradoxical dilemma for Rosa; they push her into the world of intellectualism for which she yearns, but cause her to descend into the shameful image of the "victim." Students should read the letters from Dr. Tree to discern what he represents in Rosa's life.

▶How does Dr. Tree threaten the "safety" that Rosa has established in her isolation?

▶Why does the term "survivor" threaten Rosa?

The use of Miami, Florida, as the setting for *Rosa* represents a powerful metaphor in the two stories. Ozick develops Miami as a present-day concentration camp. Students should analyze the descriptive passages of Miami for the images that represent fire, destruction, barrenness, and inhumanity. It is a life of physical and emotional deprivation. Miami becomes the inferno of the ovens in the concentration camps and the inferno in Rosa's mind. The sun burns people to "shells"; "everything is damp and shadowy." [10] The following sections should be examined closely for their representative imagery:

▶Rosa's room at the hotel (pp. 13-14)

▶Description of Florida (pp. 16–17)

▶In the restaurant with Persky (pp. 24–25)

▶The beach (p. 47)

Particular attention should be paid to the section when Rosa goes on the search for the underpants. In these passages, Ozick takes the reader to the desecrated land of the beach. The beach is the landscape of the death camps; it represents the wasteland of humanity. The barbed-wire gates and the inferno of the hotel's lower kitchens create a parallel image to the ovens of the camps. A devastating paranoia for Rosa parallels her past terror of the camps. Betrayed by the clerk Finkelstein, she is caught in the moral and ethical dilemmas of the Holocaust. This setting becomes the landscape of the camp's incarceration and the summoning of reality for Rosa. Students should discuss how the search on the beach is one of the primary motivators pushing Rosa into a different state of being:

▶What does Rosa learn about herself that night?

▶What changes are enacted after that night on the beach? Why?

## Part Three: Life Before, During, and After

"My Warsaw isn't your Warsaw." [11]

Ozick introduces the character Mr. Persky as a foil to Rosa. The development of his character becomes the catalyst of memory recovered, reality revealed, and imagination challenged. The "commonness" of Persky reveals Rosa's past, and it is through his sense of humanity that Rosa gains insight into the present and hope for the future. By looking carefully at the dialogue between these characters students can discover Rosa's past life—both real and imagined:

▶ What is "Rosa's Warsaw," and how does it distinguish itself from Persky's?

▶ What are the specific details of life in Warsaw prior to and during the war?

▶ Define the influences of education and assimilation in Rosa's life versus the "ordinariness" of Persky.

▶ What characterizes the reality and the fantasy of Rosa's past? How do we gain understanding of her suffering before the war?

▶ How is the fantasy of Magda reflective of Rosa's dreams and aspirations as a young woman?

Because of the developing relationship between Persky and Rosa, we are able to see movement in her grasp of reality. The present is revealed for its isolation and anger, and the future holds a weakening of the power of the shawl as Rosa moves slowly into the real world with Persky as her guide.

## Part Four: Religious and Social Philosophies

"Cultivation, old civilization, beauty, history!" [12]

*Rosa* allows Ozick to explore several ideologies that shape, define, and distort Rosa's life. Students should focus on the following areas in understanding the character Rosa:

▶ Define the Eightfold Path and Four Principle Truths of Buddhism. What relationship do these philosophies have to both Rosa's past and present?

▶ Define Rosa's view of life in Miami as a degrading social circumstance.

▶ Define Dr. Tree's philosophies on survivors and "consummated indifference." [13]

▶ Rosa's views on Zionism v. Nationalism (p. 40)

▶ Rosa's view of the "New World" (p. 42)

▶ Persky's philosophy, "For everything there's a bad way of describing, also a good way." [14]

## Presentation Ideas

1. Students can read supplemental stories to form a basis of comparison and research the similarities and differences in writing style, use of language, detail, voice, and description. They should present these comparative stories to the class. (See Suggested Reading.)

2. Upon the advance of allied troops to the concentration camps, the Germans began the forced marches from one camp to the next. Students should research survivors' experiences of these marches and present to the class maps, testimonies, and stories about these days of terror and survival.

3. Services were provided to refugees and survivors of World War II. Students could divide into small groups and research the social services both in Europe and the United States. How did the immigration laws of the United States affect the relocation of Jews from the camps? Each group should make presentations.

4. During World War II, many Jewish children throughout Europe were hidden from their German captors. Students should read accounts of the hidden children and develop Ozick's example of life before, during, and after for a class presentation. These accounts should be shared with the class.

## Writing Ideas

1. In both Judith Isaacson's *Seed of Sarah* and Ozick's *Rosa*, the characters immigrate to the United States after the war. Students could write a comparative essay about the two experiences. What differentiates their "adjustments" to the New World?

2. Using comparative essay form, students could write about the voice of accurate observation in *Seed of Sarah* as opposed to the metaphoric style of Ozick. How do fiction and personal testimony present two different versions of the Holocaust? What is the impact on the reader?

3. The predominant metaphor in *The Shawl* and *Rosa* is the shawl. Students should make a detailed list of the references to the shawl and its relationship to the three characters. This list can be continuous throughout the reading of both stories in order to catalog the development of characters through the shawl's changing position in the story.

4. A creative writing opportunity from *The Shawl* comes from the genre of metaphoric writing. Students should create a portfolio of creative pieces with examples of poetry, personal essay, fiction, and art work that use metaphor/analogy as the genre. This metaphoric representation could also be done in a visual art form with painting, drawing, collage, or sculpture.

5. Letter writing is a creative and informative way for a writer to draw out a story's details and reveal the development of characters. Students might compose a correspondence between two fictional or real characters. These writings should create a separate persona of the characters with special emphasis on tone, mood, and style.

## Suggested Reading

Appleman, Alicia. *Alicia: My Story*. New York: Bantam Books, 1988.

Baron, Salo W. "From a Historians Notebook." *Out of the Whirlwind*, Albert H. Friedlander, ed. New York: Schocken Books, 1976.

Eitinger, Leo. "Holocaust Survivors in the Past and Present," *The Holocaust and History*. Michael Berenbaum and Abraham Peck, eds. Bloomington and Urbana: Indiana University Press, 1998.

Hilberg, Raul. *The Destruction of the European Jews*. 3 volumes. rev. ed. New York: Holmes and Meier, 1985.

Michaels, Anne. *Fugitive Pieces*. New York: Vintage International, 1998.

Peck, Jean. *At the Fire's Center*. Bloomington and Urbana: University of Illinois Press, 1998.

Weinstein, Frida Scheps. *A Hidden Childhood*. New York: Farrar, Straus, and Giroux, Inc. 1985.

---

[1] Francine Prose, (*New York Times Book Review*, 9/10/89, section 7), p. 1.
[2] Cynthia Ozick, *The Shawl* (New York: Vintage Press, 1980), p. 4.
[3] Ibid., p. 6.
[4] Ibid., p. 10.
[5] Ibid., p. 47.
[6] Ibid., p. 14.
[7] Ibid., p. 34.
[8] Ibid., p. 69.
[9] Ibid., p. 15.
[10] Ibid., p. 16.
[11] Ibid., p. 19.
[12] Ibid., p. 21.
[13] Ibid., p. 38.
[14] Ibid., p. 56.

# Maus ——————————————————————

Art Spiegelman. Maus: A Survivor's Tale. I: My Father Bleeds History
(New York: Pantheon Books), 1973. ISBN 0-39474723-2.

### Character List

Vladek Spiegelman
Art Spiegelman
Anja Spiegelman
Mala Spiegelman

### Plot Summary

The graphic memoir *Maus* is a creative narrative by Art Spiegelman that redefines the genre of Holocaust literature. Written as a narrative comic book, *Maus* portrays Eastern European Jews as mice, Germans as cats, and Poles as pigs. Relying on the metaphor of the pursuit of cat and mouse, Spiegelman develops these characters with careful attention to the events of the Holocaust. The narrative is the personal testimony of Spiegelman's father, a prisoner of war and inmate of Auschwitz during World War II. The graphic novel takes the reader from the early days of occupied Poland to contemporary life in New York City.

A child of Holocaust survivors is often referred to as a second-generation survivor, and it is in this voice that Spiegelman illustrates his relationship with his father. As a second-generation survivor, Spiegelman comments upon and gives insight into this tenuous relationship between father and son. He records the difficulties of living with survivors under the strain of their memories and experiences of war.

This book provides a unique look at creating metaphor through art. The illustrations complement the narrative text. Because it is written in comic-book form, the language is concise and spare. The artwork enhances and develops the emotion and meaning.

In discussing this story, it is important to see the interaction between art, language, and experience. Students will become aware of the interplay between the three voices and the effect this has upon recording personal testimony with historical data. The discussion of each chapter will be based upon three elements: personal testimony, second-generation experience, and visual art.

## Objectives for Teaching *Maus*

The graphic novel *Maus* provides a unique study of the use of metaphor and imagery to depict the historical, ethical, and emotional experiences of the Holocaust. The following objectives give a foundation for an understanding of the text and graphics:

▶ To examine text for historical documentation of the Holocaust
▶ To study the narrative voice of personal testimony
▶ To understand the voice of second-generation survivors
▶ To study art as metaphor

As students study this graphic story, it is important for them to consider the following questions:

▶ How is the language of the narrative reflected in the illustrations?
▶ In drawing a storyboard comic, why and how must the author/artist consider the sequence of events?
▶ If you were to summarize the message of each chapter, what would it be?
▶ How does Spiegelman invoke the emotion of the Holocaust through his illustrations and testimony?

## Opening Pages: The Past

From the opening pages, Spiegelman carefully begins to weave together the three elements of this book. The introductory pages introduce Spiegelman as a young child in Rego Park, New York. The interaction between the child and the father immediately sets the stage for the development of their relationship. Distressed by the insults of his friends, Spiegelman goes to his father for comfort. Spiegelman uses the narrative design of these pages to help illustrate the characters of child and father. The picture of the father standing over a workbench establishes him as a laborer, a man who is capable and determined. When the boy looks to his father for sympathy, he is greeted in a harsh tone of instruction and admonishment: "Friends? Your friends? If you lock them together in a room for a week . . . then you could see what it is, friends!"[1] This single sentence and illustration shows the power of the father. His words echo terrible experiences from the past. The father's cryptic and strong messages negate the young boy's own experience, for what could ever be as terrible as hiding from the Nazis?

The language and artwork of these opening pages establishes the inflection of both father and son. The outrage versus the yearning for understanding characterizes these two voices and continues throughout the telling of the story. Spiegelman uses the caption boxes in a measured manner reflecting each spoken word in the illustrations. The use of pen and ink mirrors the art produced in the concentration camps. The lack of color reinforces the darkness of the message. It also allows for play between the setting detail and the characters. Spiegelman's meticulous background detail is illustrated in the drawings on page 6. The picture of the young boy, dressed in suspenders and carrying strap roller skates, places the narrative in a specific time and place. The detail of the row houses shows the suburban world of New York during the 1950s.

## Chapter One: The Sheik

"I was at that time, a young and really a nice, handsome boy."[2]

The first chapter of this book provides background information to establish the facts of the past. Because graphic narrative is limited in its use of detailed language, the important elements of the story must be revealed with a minimum of words. Spiegelman gives the reader three significant pieces of information in the opening blocks: he has not seen his father in a long time; his mother committed suicide, and his father is remarried to a woman named Mala. These facts are the threads that weave in and out of the entire story as Spiegelman embellishes on their detail through illustrative and written narrative.

Students should be aware of the events that are occurring during the time of these opening chapters. By 1933 Hitler has already established power in Germany and is beginning to change the face of Germany through the Nazi Party rule. It would be important for students to have an understanding of the early days of the Third Reich, including information on the Nuremberg Laws and the invasion of Austria, Czechoslovakia, and Poland.

Chapter One gives the reader necessary information about time and place. The father, Vladek, begins his narrative in his youthful days in Czestochowa, Poland, 1935. Painting himself as a bright, ambitious man, "The Sheik" reveals the charisma and appeal that once was. The chapter shows the life of a young boy engaged in work, love, and play, with little care for the events and dangers of Europe looming in the distance. This chapter tells the love story of Anja and Vladek, a story that helps to establish further details of life in Poland at the time. Vladek deals in textiles, and Anja's family owns several successful textile-manufacturing plants. The portrait of this family gives students an understanding of the assimilated Jews of Poland. They were significant members of the community, providing jobs for the locals. They were respected for their education and wealth. Their living conditions were comfortable, and food, education, travel, and material wealth were the foundation of their lives.

The voice of the second generation is also established in the first chapter. From Vladek's admonishment of Mala's use of a wire hanger, to the chapter's closing pages, the power and force of this character upon his son and wife is astounding. The closing pages illustrate the friction between father and son. Trying to censor what will be written about him, Vladek insists Art stick to the facts of the story. Vladek says his love affair and youthful indiscretion "has nothing to do with the Holocaust."[3] Through this exchange, the reader sees the importance of personal testimony. Spiegelman understands that the victims of the Holocaust need to be humanized, given individual identities, and not looked at as an incomprehensible mass of six million who died at the hands of the Germans. Vladek does not understand the significance of his testimony.

The illustrations of this chapter enhance the tone and mood of Vladek's text. On page 13 the father pedals furiously as the image of Rudolph Valentino looms in the background. The cameo picture on page 12 illustrates his authority and self-aggrandizement as a young man of extreme self-confidence and sexual appeal. The voice of Vladek is reflected in the illustrations as he enhances his story with movie-like images of the young girl clinging to Vladek's legs. His story of his youthful love affair is dramatized with the bold sound effects of "SLAM" and the scorned woman's weeping (page 20).

Holocaust history is also enforced through the illustrations. On page 12, Vladek's forearm is pictured with a number. This gives reference to the tattooing of camp inmates at Auschwitz-Birkenaus. The scars are physical as well as emotional and are a daily reminder of the horror of the camps. Several blocks show Vladek and his family in everyday living situations: eating an amply supplied dinner, dancing, walking in the park, talking on the telephone, embarking on trains. These common occurrences give evidence to the normality of life for the Jews before the start of the war.

## Chapter Two: The Honeymoon

"I tell you, there's a pogrom going on in Germany."[4]

The title page of this chapter gives warning to the turn of events in the narrative. The words "The Honeymoon" are insignificant compared to the flag and its display of the German swastika. This emblem was adopted in 1933 by the reigning political party, the National Socialist German Workers' Party (NAZI). With their backs to the reader, the characters see the flag as we do, looming large overhead, powerful and threatening. This is a piece of illustrative foreshadowing to the events of Chapter Two. The second chapter gives the reader the facts of the steady assault by the Poles and Germans upon the Jewish community. Although this family is wealthy and of good standing in the community, they too will suffer the injustices of the Nazis.

The early pages of the chapter give a view of the marriage of Vladek and Anja. Their love is exemplified in his devotion to her, despite anxious, emotional conditions. They have a child, Richieu. But the effects of Nazi infiltration begin to change their perspectives. Students should take careful notes of the changes that occur in both this family and community. Starting with the interrogation of Anja over the package she has hidden, the story slowly begins to reveal Nazi terrorism.

The illustrations of the sanitarium where Anja goes are explicit in giving historical documentation. Although the sanitarium is a paradise with its elaborate gardens, shops, theatre, and restaurants, the first view of the Nazi swastika looms heavy in the background of this idyllic village. Spiegelman carefully introduces the language and images of the Holocaust in these pages. Page 32 shows the black "pleasure" train going to the sanitarium, a foreboding image of the trains that will become the death vehicles for the transports. With the black swastika in the background of the blocks on page 33, Spiegelman begins to show the changes in the lives of Polish Jews. The view outside the window shows "Jude," Jew, written on the windows of Jewish-owned businesses. Spiegelman illustrates the German soldiers leading a couple out of town carrying a flag reading, "I am a filthy Jew."[5] Rumors of the confiscation of businesses and the disappearance of Jews gives historical documentation of the events of this time. Spiegelman juxtaposes the image of this couple blissfully dancing together against the news that Anja's father's factory has been robbed. The father declares this as an anti-Semitic activity, and the Spiegelman family begins to deny the reality that is surrounding them. The peaceful streets of the sanitarium become the riot-infested streets of their hometown.

The family prays the war will not enter Poland, but Vladek is drafted into the Polish Army. With the move to Sosnowiec, the saga of this testimony becomes more grim and terrifying. It is important for students to understand the significance of the annexation of Poland in terms of the development of the war. Students should consult maps showing Europe before and after the war to illustrate the magnitude of Hitler's power. An understanding of the size and significance of the Jewish population in Poland is crucial to the full appreciation of this aspect of the Holocaust. (See Research Ideas for topics of instruction.) Polish Jews suffered in great numbers under the reign of Hitler in the centrally occupied territory of Poland.

Spiegelman ends the chapter with the insights of the second-generation perspective. As Vladek complains about doctors and medicine, he retains his air of superiority. Vladek still emerges as "The Sheik," but in a more pitiful and empty way.

## Chapter Three: Prisoner of War

"I was very frightened."[6]

Just as the war begins to escalate, so do the events of the story with the drama and terror of Vladek Spiegelman's experiences. The personal testimony becomes a litany of fear and confusion as the young man struggles to survive the injustices of the prisoner of war labor camps.

Desperation becomes the emotion that Spiegelman seeks to convey. His illustrations on page 46 of the starving young Vladek, as he tries to escape the draft in 1922, are complemented by the darkness of the drawings of the trenches. Warfare becomes the background of this story, and Spiegelman uses graphic detail to sow the terror. While the Polish "pigs" loom large in the blocks, the character Vladek becomes small and insignificant. He is shown hiding in the rushes, face darkened by fear, his view limited by the scope of his rifle. The immediacy and detail of these drawings pull the reader into the emotion of the moment. As the shots from Vladek's gun explode, so do the illustrations. The block of the German soldier is graphic in its sound effects and movement. The soldier is obliterated by the explosion but humanized with his single hand ascending for help (p. 48).

Vladek's story then becomes a foreshadowing of the experiences of the concentration camps. It is through these pages that Spiegelman explores the atrocities of the labor camps. The German soldiers rule with supreme and cruel authority. Their faces are menacing, and the darkness of their uniform makes them imposing figures. The conditions of the camp are illustrated with tents, barbed wire, and armed patrol guards. Spiegelman also emphasizes the irony of choice. To volunteer is a dangerous and uncertain future, but to remain is sure death by starvation and disease. The choices for the prisoners and later the Jews were limited to one form or another of torture. On page 54 Spiegelman displays the sign announcing positions for labor camp work. With its tempting promise of food and shelter, Vladek volunteers. The artist emphasizes the irony of this situation. The war effort is supported by the labor of the enemy; they produce the munitions and build the roads that aid the transport of the Jews to the camps. And although Vladek is still beaten, he is grateful for clean sheets and cots. He states, "There was enough to eat, and a warm bed. It was better to stay."[7]

The depth of this metaphoric narrative is evident when Spiegelman introduces in the dream sequence some important elements of the Jewish religion. When Vladek is visited in a dream by his dead grandfather, he is given the assurance, "You will come out of this place—free! On the day of Parshas Truma."[8] The significance of this passage from the Bible reflects the faith of Vladek in the God of the Old Testament. The *Parshas Truma* is found in the book of Exodus 25:19–27. God commands the Jewish people to build a sanctuary that will serve as a worship center for his chosen people. The passage details specific instructions for the construction of the ark where the tablets of the Ten Commandments will be kept. The building of the tabernacle symbolizes the presence of God within the community. It acts as the holiest of places in the Jewish nation and is a constant reminder of the power of God. In the dream, the grandfather delivers this prophecy to his grandson. He is drawn with a prayer shawl or *tallit* and phylactery on his forehead. The phylactery is a leather box containing the prayer Shema, the call to worship God. (See Poetry chapter for further analysis.) It is tightly bound to the forehead and forearm with leather straps. The reference to the holy center of worship, the presence of the god-like power of the grandfather, the tallit and phylactery show the faith Vladek still embraces despite the hardship of his life. These symbols all emphasize the presence of God in the concentration camps. Parshas Truma represents the hope and promise of the rise of the Jewish nation. Like the prophecies that come to the forefathers of the Jewish religion, the reading of this passage of scripture is the omen of a future for the Spiegelman family. The legacy lives in the events of hope and promise of this family: Vladek's release from the labor camp, the marriage of Anja and Vladek, and Spiegelman's birth and bar mitzvah.

The narrative illustrations of this chapter reinforce the significance of the events of the war. Spiegelman carefully manipulates images to create metaphor and meaning. On page 58 Spiegelman draws a column of faceless prisoners. These men are indistinguishable from each other; the obliteration of their features mirrors the denial of individualism by the Nazi Party in the camps. Spiegelman craftily uses the size of the cartoon blocks to emphasize meaning; combining story with emotion, the illustration on page 60 of the map of Poland dominates. Page 61 gives the reader a horrifying view of the death marches and cruelties of the Germans: the guards line up a group of prisoners for execution, delight clear on the soldiers' faces. The risk of a simple human act of urination is emphasized (page 62) as well as the profound pleasure of a piece of chocolate. Spiegelman also implies meaning with the introduction of the "mask" on the characters' faces. The false front of Vladek as a Polish citizen (symbolized by the pig face) shows the need to fit in and become a face in a crowd in order to prevent special attention.

With Vladek's return from the prison camps, he receives news of what life has been like in his hometown. Students should read pages 65–66 for the historical information provided:

▶The shaving of Vladek's father's beard

▶The roundup and harassment of Jews in the streets

▶The confiscation of the seltzer factory

▶The imposition of curfew

Spiegelman is setting the stage for the next episode of the journey with this information of the imposed restrictions on the Jews.

The chapter ends with a disturbing incident between father and son. The frustration and anger Spiegelman felt as a child is mirrored in these closing blocks. Spiegelman's father throws his son's coat away in the trash inciting Art's feelings of confusion and disbelief. The father's inability to let his thirty-year-old son make even the simplest decisions emphasizes the strains of their relationships. As a survivor, Vladek's control of his son and wife are paramount. The dejection Spiegelman feels at this realization is illustrated in the last block: with head down, wearing the out-of-fashion jacket his father has given him, the dejected Spiegelman declares, "I just can't believe it. . . ."[9] The confusion for second-generation survivors is characterized by this despair: fear and astonishment at what their parents have survived and the effects of these experiences upon them as children of survivors.

## Chapter Four: The Noose Tightens

"And so we lived for more than a year. But always things came a little worse, a little worse. . . ."[10]

The illustrations and narrative of Chapter Four complement each other to give students a clear idea of how the Germans terrorized the Jews of Poland. As Vladek's testimony continues, the backdrop of the drawings gives face to the terror and danger of those years. With twelve men, women, and children living under one roof, conditions for the family become increasingly difficult. Spiegelman records the facts of the war: the imposition of ration cards, the dealings of the black market, the threat of labor camps, the confiscation of material goods, the lack of income, and the world of bribery and lies. The lie of the camp Theresienstadt as a "convalescent home" is revealed, as is the importance of the Judenrat or Jewish Council (pages 73–79.) Spiegelman's drawings take on special significance in these pages. Students should examine carefully the message and significance of the following blocks:

▶The roundup and beatings of Jews (p. 80)

▶The isolation and fear of Vladek (Jewish star block, p. 80)

▶The formation of the ghetto (p. 82)

▶The hangings (p. 83)

▶The darkness, guilt, and despair of Vladek and his family (p. 84)

Pages 89–90 give witness to the terrible methods of the Nazi Party. With accurate detail, Spiegelman shows the roundup of 25,000 Jews in the stadium. The passport with its "J" for Juden, the barbed wire, the orders to the right and left, the rumors and reality of Auschwitz, the separation of families is all given in explicit and moving detail. Perhaps the most moving of these pictures is the small block on page 91. Here Spiegelman gives us insight into the physical and emotional exhaustion of his father in recalling these memories. The frenzy of the bicycle pedaling comes to a stop with Vladek's dizziness, and the reader sees only a deflated old man. Spiegelman also gives another voice to this testimony with the affirmation by Mala of the horrors of the roundup.

Mala's testimony is overshadowed by the fear of disturbing Vladek's sense of "order." As Art searches for his mother's missing diaries, the reader sees fear is still a legacy of the Nazis that haunts this family.

## Chapter Five: Mouse Holes

The voice of the second-generation survivor emerges in full force in this chapter of *Maus*. Spiegelman tells a story within a story when he introduces the history of his earlier comic book, *Prisoner on the Hell Planet*. This graphic book reveals the mental anguish experienced by Spiegelman at the suicide of his mother. The characters are drawn with exaggerated form and facial expression emphasizing meaning. Spiegelman depicts himself emerging from a state mental hospital in striped prison garb, creating the metaphor of his imprisonment by his life of trauma. Students should look carefully at the illustrations of this section of *Maus*. Both Spiegelman and his father are depicted in their anguish with the close-up detail of the son's face and the death-like mask of the father (pages 99–100). Vladek is pictured hollow-eyed, desperate, and lost. These pages give insight into the lives of children of survivors. In the illustrations, the casket is enlarged with the screams of the father imposed upon the background of the drawings. The torment Spiegelman feels at his mother's death is characterized by the block on page 103 of his interior mind. Words of guilt are superimposed upon visions from his childhood: the child in prison clothes being read to, piles of dead bodies before a wall with the swastika, and his mother's tattooed arm with the razor blade upon the wrist. Spiegelman packs in the images of guilt and confusion ending with the symbolic drawings of his incarceration in a prison cell. With the accusatory words, "You murdered me, Mommy, and you left me here to take the rap!!!"[11] Spiegelman characterizes the plight of those left to live the memories of the dead.

The latter half of this chapter of *Maus* details episode after episode of sorrow and loss for the Spiegelman family. Spiegelman writes of the move to the ghetto in Srodula, the forced labor in German "shops," and the constant hiding in bunkers. The story's pace is fast and complex in its illustrative images. Each block reveals a new and terrifying aspect of life for the Jews of Poland. Students should read this chapter with close attention to the artwork. Barbed wire, bold signs, armed guards, attack dogs, gated ghettos, faces of despair and determination characterize the story in these pages. On page 108 Spiegelman portrays the brutal murder of children at the hands of the Nazis. The block illustrating this is carefully drawn with the child's head off the picture and the force of the Nazi's action as the emphasis. The hiding and eventual killing of Richieu and the other children is exemplified with the ferocity of Tosha's declaration, "No! I won't go to their gas chambers. And my children won't go to their gas chambers."[12]

The life of hiding is meticulously drawn showing crowded and desperate conditions. And as Spiegelman reveals the difficulties of surviving these times, the anguish of the family is characterized in the drawings. Students should give a close examination of the following blocks in analyzing historical data, narrative voice, and illustrative metaphor:

▶The deportation of Anja's father (p. 115)

▶The threat of deportation (p. 121)

▶The path to Sosnowiec with the sign of the swastika (p. 125)

This chapter begins with an unsympathetic view of Vladek, the pecuniary man who risks his life to climb on a roof to save money. But Spiegelman gives a different view of his father at the close of the chapter. The revelation of the jewelry and artifacts hidden in Srodula during the war affects both father and son. With incredulity at these found objects, Spiegelman comforts the agitated and lost man his father has become. As the facts of Vladek's life are revealed to the son, there is a tone of better understanding between them.

## Chapter Six: Mouse Trap

"Thank God there are still some kind people left. I thought. . . ."[13]

Chapter Five of *Maus* ends with Vladek's complaints about his present wife Mala, and the final chapter begins with her complaints against him. The coupling of the complaints questions the quality of life for these two survivors. But the closing pages of this graphic novel take the reader more deeply into the memories and the real horror of their past. With determination to survive, Vladek and Anja travel back to Sosnowiec to find shelter from old "friends" and acquaintances. Spiegelman draws the couple with the Polish "pig masks" to emphasize the conditions these two must endure. With constant surveillance by the Nazis, the Spiegelmans must hide their Jewishness. As they try to save themselves, they hide in a barn and a rat-filled cellar. Spiegelman gives homage to the "righteous few" who aided Jews at this time despite the risks to their personal safety. Dealing in the black market and trading jewelry for food become the methods of survival, until the promise of escaping to Hungary is a viable choice.

The last blocks of this chapter reveal the foreboding and terror of these final days for the Spiegelmans. Departing on the train for the promise of a safe life, their travels are stopped with the arrest on the train. Spiegelman draws the characters in silhouette being marched to prison by the Germans. The final block of this episode is the largest of the novel. The gateposts of Auschwitz-Birkenau are depicted with the insignia "*Arbeit Macht Frei*, Work Will Make You Free." Vladek says, "We knew the stories—that they will gas us and throw us in the ovens. This was 1944. . . . We knew everything. And here we were."[14] This ends the personal testimony by Spiegelman's father of his life in Poland.

The final pages of this graphic novel return us to the conflict between father and son. Art pleads with his father to find his mother's diaries from the war only to be told that his father has burned them. Like the fires of the Holocaust, the burning of the diaries represents for the son the destruction of memory and honor for his mother. As Spiegelman walks away from his father, the final word spoken is "Murderer."[15]

The complexity of this story continues with this somewhat incomplete ending. Spiegelman subsequently wrote a sequel to this novel titled *Maus II.* When asked about the experience of interviewing his father and working on *Maus* for thirteen years, Spiegelman responded, "Maybe this was a way of maintaining the relationship with him. In fact, in many ways I have a better relationship with him now than I did when he was alive." [16] The legacy and importance of personal testimony lives in these words for all readers of Holocaust literature.

**Presentation Ideas**

1. *Maus* provides students significant information about moral and ethical choices. Broader writing and discussion of goals could focus on the political power of individuals and government, the rights of individuals in totalitarian governments, racism, or prejudices. Students could plan a panel discussion on these topics to share with other classes studying similar issues.
2. There is considerable controversy about the use of animals to depict the injustices of the Holocaust. Critics say that Spiegelman himself encourages stereotyping in his depiction of the Jews as timid mice, the Germans as ferocious cats, and the Poles as stupid pigs. Students could research the book reviews and interviews with Spiegelman and conduct their own debate over this issue. (See Internet Sources at end of chapter.)
3. Comic books have a long literary history. Students could research the start of this art genre and what place it holds in contemporary art and writing.

**Writing and Visual Art Ideas**

The reading and study of *Maus* provides a number of thoughtful writing and visual art projects for students of all levels. The simplicity of the written text and the detail of the graphic text allow students to find meaning in not only the experience of the Holocaust but their own lives as well. With the artwork as important as the text, these projects give students of varying abilities an opportunity to explore graphic storytelling. The writing helps students discover the genres of historical, personal, and political writing.

1. The use of animals as characters in narrative is a commonly used writing style. Parables from all cultures and time periods exist: Aesop's fables, the Greek myths, Native American folklore, Norse adventures, African folktales, and many more. Working either in small groups or individually, students should research and read several different myths of diverse cultural backgrounds. Choosing one story, students should write and design a graphic book of their chosen myth. Teachers may break this lesson into several parts:

    ▶ The research and reading of the myths and fables
    ▶ The rewriting of the myth in language that would accompany a graphic novel (dialogue, description, narrative voice, inner voice)
    ▶ The design of a storyboard: blocks for the graphics and the text (this can be done on computer, also)
    ▶ Combining text and graphics to tell the story.

    Teachers should consider materials and format for this project. Students who lack confidence in their artistic skills can use collage, color block representation, textual fonts, and children's drawings. Emphasis for this project should be on the marriage of graphics and text. Students should consider the following questions when working on their project:

▶ What are the most important elements of this story that need to be read and seen?

▶ What graphic images will best represent the personalities of the characters?

▶ Have I considered sequence, background, and foreground?

2. Personal testimony is one of the most significant elements of *Maus*. This makes the story a perfect model for autobiographical writing. Students should read small anecdotal sections of the graphic book: the introductory pages, the story of Vladek's love affair, the visit to the sanitarium, the view from the trains, the hiding in the bunkers, and the actions of the Germans in Srodula. Then focusing on a single memory from their pasts, students should write a personal essay. Following the same outline above, students should write, reduce, revise, draw, and create the graphics, and then combine the two for a personal graphic book.

3. *Maus* is not only the story of the Holocaust but also an examination of the relationship between father and son. Using a fictional voice, students could write a short story characterizing a relationship between fathers, mothers, and their children. This story could also become a graphic novella.

4. Historical fiction lends itself well to graphic design. Students could choose an important historical event and write a story that would provide clear and graphic accuracy of the event. This story could also become a graphic novella.

5. Political cartooning as propaganda was an important element in World War II. Students should research both German and American artwork of this time period. Choosing an important contemporary political issue, students could design their own propaganda poster. Students could also use this forum to express political opinion and satire.

6. Listening to personal testimony on tape or computer is an important way for students to learn about the Holocaust. Using the Yale University Fortunoff Video Library on computer, or watching the film documentaries *Shoah* or *Maine Survivors Remember the Holocaust* would provide students the rich opportunity to put voice and face to personal testimony. Students could then create graphic novels of one of the stories they studied and listened to or watched.

7. Students could read Spiegelman's *Maus II, a Survivor's Tale: And Here My Troubles Began*. Comparing the narrative text and graphic design of this later work, students could write reviews of both books.

## Suggested Reading

Dreifus, Claudia. "Art Spiegelman: The Progressive Interview." *Progressive* 53 (Nov. 1989), pp. 34–37.

Spiegelman, Art. *Maus II, a Survivor's Tale: And Here My Troubles Began.* New York: Pantheon, 1992.

Tabachnick, Stephen E., "Of Maus and Memory: The Structure of Art Spiegelman's Graphic Novel of the Holocaust." *Image: A Journal of Verbal Visual Enquiry* 9:2 (1993), pp. 154–62.

Witek, Joseph. *Comic Books as History: The Narrative Art of Jack Jackson, Art Spiegelman, and Harvey Pekar.* Jackson: University of Mississippi, 1989.

## Internet Sources

www.voyager.learntech.com/catalogu/mau/indepth

www.uidaho.edu/~thomas/English_501/Maus.html

www.geocities.com/Area51/Zone/9923/ispieg2.html

[1] Art Spiegelman, *Maus: A Survivor's Tale. I: My Father Bleeds History* (New York: Pantheon Books, 1973), p. 6.

[2] Ibid., p. 13.

[3] Ibid., p. 23.

[4] Ibid., p. 33.

[5] Ibid.

[6] Ibid., p. 62.

[7] Ibid., p. 56.

[8] Ibid., p. 57.

[9] Ibid., p. 69.

[10] Ibid., p. 79.

[11] Ibid., p. 103.

[12] Ibid., p. 109.

[13] Ibid., p. 137.

[14] Ibid., p. 157.

[15] Ibid., p. 159.

[16] http://www.geocities.com/Area51/Zone/9923/ispieg2.html

Books

# Poetry of the Holocaust _____

Poetry

## Glossary

**Accent.** The emphasis on a word or syllable

**Alliteration.** The repetition of a consonant sound; example: softly, sounded sighs

**Analogy.** A comparison of two or more things of similar characteristics

**Chapbook.** A small book of stories, essays, or poems designed and published by the author

**Free verse.** Lines of poetry that are not strictly metered or rhymed

**Imagery.** Literary or artistic expression with rich and complex details of ideas, objects, and feelings

**Metaphor.** A single word or phrase in which a name or a quality is attributed to something which is not directly applicable; example: nerves of steel

**Pace.** Pattern and speed of language

**Rhyme.** Agreement in the sound of words or syllables

**Rhythm.** The measured pace of a line of poetry

**Simile.** A comparison using "like" or "as"

**Stanza.** A group of lines of verse

**Symbol.** Something used to represent an idea, emotion, or event

## Introduction

The use of poetry to teach the Holocaust is a marvelous tool for teachers. Poetry by Holocaust survivors and those who perished in the concentration camps provides a historical perspective on the events of World War II. With its richness of language and imagery, poetry elicits emotion and reaction from students. Poetry also delivers its message with an economy of language making it accessible to all reading levels. The study of poetry allows a multitude of writing opportunities for students.

It is essential for teachers to make the understanding of the events of the Holocaust clear to the students before teaching this unit. Poetry provides a richness

118

of experience, but one that must come in context with the larger themes of the Holocaust. Because of the autobiographical nature of poetry, it is often useful for students to have background information on the author.

The poetry chosen for this unit should be distinguished from poetry written *about* the Holocaust by authors who did not directly experience the events of the Holocaust. The poetry is presented in chronological order to events of the Holocaust.

## Suggestions for Teaching Poetry

It is important for teachers to dispel the myth that poetry is secretive, overly personal, and impossible to decipher. In order to have students embrace poetry, teachers should make language usage and meaning, style, and theme completely understandable. The following suggestions are made to help in the *process* of teaching and understanding a poem:

1. Every student should have a copy of the poem before them to facilitate marking significant lines and ideas.
2. Take several minutes for the students to read the poem silently at least two times. Have students mark important ideas, questions, or specific lines they would like to discuss.
3. The poem should be read aloud by two students at separate times. Teachers should try to choose students who have different oral reading styles.
4. A discussion of unfamiliar vocabulary will help in the understanding of the poem.
5. The students should then read the poem to themselves one more time, underlining a significant line or lines or a phrase or passage that moves them in some way or raises a question. Going around in a circle, students should read aloud their selections. Students should be encouraged to read their lines despite the possible repetition by other students. No responses or talking should take place in the circle beyond the reading and repetition of lines. Explain it is voice you are investigating, as well as meaning.
6. Discussion of the poem can begin with plot summary: Who is the speaker? Who is she/he addressing? Where does the poem take place? When?
7. The students are now ready to discuss the meaning of the poem. Teachers should encourage the students to search for the questions the poem poses: What is the conflict? What emotions are evident? What is the message the author wants to leave with the reader?
8. Discussion of style often accompanies the meaning of a poem. Teachers should ask: How does this author create the mood and meaning of the poem? What metaphors and imagery are used? How does the form of the poem reflect its content? (Free or metered, rhyming or non-rhyming, line breaks, capitalization, punctuation.)
9. At the end of the discussion, the poem should be read aloud one more time, with a discussion of the difference in meaning from the first silent reading.

## General Writing Ideas

After discussion, these writing ideas can be used to further understanding of the poem:

▶ Instruct students to underline one line or several sequential lines of the

poem written in an imagistic style. Have students write their understanding of this line or passage in one, complete sentence.

▶ Underline all the nouns in the poem. Have students replace original
  nouns for ones of their choice. How does this change affect the
  meaning and voice of the poem? Why?

▶ In discussing the style of the poem, teachers should emphasize line
  starts and stops and punctuation. Have students choose a section and
  alter the line starts and stops. How does this affect the meaning and
  impact of the language?

▶ Students can write a poem of their own modeling the style and language
  use of the poem being studied. Choosing a subject matter of their choice,
  they should be prepared to discuss the meaning and style of their poem.

▶ Each student could create a chapbook of his/her poetry. (See Glossary
  of Terms for this chapter.) This handmade book can include artistic
  representations of the poetry. For students proficient with computer
  graphics, font styles and form can be explored.

For further instruction on how to teach poetry, see Suggested Reading.

## Death Fugue — Paul Celan

### Analysis of "Death Fugue"

*Webster's Encyclopedic Dictionary* defines a fugue as "a musical composition in
which the melody (theme) is taken up by successive voices in imitation, so that
the original melody seems to be pursued by its counterpoints."[1] Celan uses this
model of a musical style to craft his poem "Death Fugue." The metaphor of the
poem reiterates the "melody" or theme of a dance of death. Analysis of the
poem relates directly to the composite of musical imagery throughout the
poem.

The first stanza of the poem lays the foundation for the pattern and theme.
Celan introduces the narrator's voice in the first lines and follows with an alter-
nating voice of the overseer. These two voices "chase" each other throughout the
composition. One voice expresses the despair and relentless conditions he faces,
while the voice of the observer is relentless in its brutality and violence. These two
voices weave in and out of each other in repetition and synthesis of voice. They
are the principal dancers in this fugue, joined in the voice of death. Celan pro-
poses a paradox in this twinning. The voice of the laborer is imagistic and
complicated in its symbols while the casual violence of the observer is heard in a
sardonic but forcefully clear tone. These two tones paint the portrait of opposing

## Death Fugue

Black milk of daybreak we drink it at sundown
we drink it at noon in the morning we drink it at night
we drink and we drink it
we dig a grave in the breezes there one lies unconfined
A man lives in the house he plays with the serpents he writes
he writes when the dusk falls to Germany your golden hair
      Margarete
He writes it and steps out of doors and the stars are flashing he
      whistles his pack out
he whistles his Jews out in earth has them dig for a grave
he commands us strike up for the dance

Black milk of daybreak we drink you at night
We drink in the morning at noon we drink you at sundown
we drink and we drink you
A man lives in the house he plays with the serpents he writes
he writes when the dusk falls to Germany your golden hair
      Margarete
your ashen hair Shulamith we dig a grave in the breezes there
      one lies unconfined

He calls out jab deeper into the earth you lot you others sing now
      and play
he grabs at the iron in his belt he waves it his eyes are blue
jab deeper your lot with your spades you others play on for the
      dance

Black milk of daybreak we drink you at night
we drink you at noon in the morning we drink you at sundown
we drink and we drink you
a man lives in the house your golden hair Margarete
your ashen hair Shulamith he plays with the serpents
he calls out more sweetly play death death is a master from
      Germany
he calls out more darkly now stroke your strings then as smoke
      you will rise into air
then a grave you will have in the clouds there one lies unconfined

Black milk of daybreak we drink you at night
We drink you at noon death is a master from Germany
we drink you at sundown and in the morning we drink and we
      drink you
death is a master from Germany his eyes are blue
he strikes you with leaden bullets his aim is true
a man lives in the house your golden hair Margarete
he sets his pack on to us he grants us a grave in the air
he plays with the serpents and daydreams death is a master from
      Germany

your golden hair Margarete
your ashen hair Shulamith[2]

—Paul Celan

images and are developed from the first line of the poem to the end.

The first stanza also creates the pattern of the lines. The narrator begins the poem with the confusing and opposing images of "Black milk of daybreak"(l.1). The commonly accepted image of daybreak as an awakening or rebirth is completely dispelled with the image of blackness. Sundown and noon are defined in the same terms stressing the persistence of blackness through the course of a day. The pleasure of a sunset is displaced by the imagery of evil and pain. Celan uses the word "milk" to support the opposing images. This is not milk of sustenance, but a poisoned substance, darkened by the evil surrounding the laborers.

The poem continues to give the reader the setting and events of this single moment in time that perpetuates itself over and over again. The laborers are digging a grave for "one unconfined" (l.4). This is a strong image for readers and is taut with interpretive meaning. In the Jewish religion, it is believed that to bury a body is an act of ultimate goodness (a *mitzvah*). Burial rites are strictly observed: a body must be prepared immediately for an expedient burial, for to lie "unconfined" prevents the sanctity of burial. This single corpse of the poem is representative of the countless victims of the Holocaust who were denied the rites of a holy burial. The voice of the overseer then infiltrates this image as he "plays with the serpents" (l.5). His "playing," as with an orchestra, reinforces the fugue theme, but also acts as a voice of complete disregard for human suffering. The laborers are instruments the overseer uses to entertain himself. The analogy to the serpent develops the theme of the Jews as the ultimate creation of evil to the Nazis.

A new element is then introduced into the fugue with the reference to "your golden hair Margarete" (l.7). Margarete becomes a poetic symbol of beauty and innocence in opposition to the horror surrounding her. She is the perfect blond Aryan portrayed in opposition to the Jew Shulamith. As the overseer "whistles his Jews out" like a pack of animals, he is whistling his theme of death "for the dance" (l.8–9). The use of a new element in each stanza surrounded by the refrain of "black milk" continues throughout the poem.

The second stanza of the poem is the repetition of the refrain. This voice creates the elegiac tone of the poem. The enunciation of repeated words is a model of the prayer for the dead recited by Jews. This prayer, the Kaddish, is recited by a gathering of ten people (a *minyan)* who constitute a community to honor the dead. This prayer is chanted in song three times each day at dawn, noon, and sunset for one year. This same community of mourning becomes the group who digs the graves and grieves the death of the victims of the Holocaust. The new element of this stanza is the line "your ashen hair Shulamith" (l.16). With the reference of ashen versus golden hair, Shulamith presents an opposing image to Margarete. The deathly pale of ashen suggests the ash of the "unconfined" exterminated in the death camp crematoria. These two are joined in a minyan as both the mourners and victims.

The next stanza belongs solely to the overseer. He orders the laborers to "dig deeper you lot you others sing now/and play" (l.19). He becomes the quintessential leader of this orchestra of death. His Aryan superiority is evident in the blueness of his eyes and "the iron belt" of the Nazi Party (l.20). The violence of this stanza counters the solemnity of the previous lines.

In the fourth stanza, the lines mimic the "chasing" style of the musical fugue. Here the refrain is heard again, and the new elements are interwoven into each other in an intricate pattern. The serpent joins with Shulamith as the voice of the overseer comes "more sweetly," and he is now the "master" of this dance (l.28–29). The new element of the smoke in this stanza becomes the reference to the crematoria of the death camps. Now the theme of unconfined becomes an ethereal image. The bodies are released but still unconfined.

The tone of the poem changes in the next stanza. The refrain is repeated, but the urgency of the theme becomes apparent with the new element. The violence of the overseer is more tangible with his "bullets" and "true aim" (l.38). Celan depicts this murderer as one who "sets his pack on to us he grants us a grave in the air" (l.40). The pack is the burden of murder and complicity of the Nazis in the killing of their victims. The verbs in this stanza—"strikes," "grants," "plays," "sets," "daydreams"—all move the poem to its final lines and imagery.

With the refrain of Margarete and Shulamith, the poet returns the reader to the recitation of the theme of death and mourning. The calling of names is the final tribute of the Kaddish as the dead are remembered for all time.

Paul Celan continued to write poetry about his experiences of the Holocaust after his escape from the labor camps. Students should read several other selections by Celan to gain a further understanding of this style and intent of meaning.

## Writing Ideas

1. The use of repetition is an important tool for poets. Repeating a line emphasizes its importance and establishes a rhythm in the reading of a poem. Where and when the line is repeated also establishes the tone and mood of a poem. Students should compose a single line that characterizes the theme for an original poem. When they have crafted the best line to express their main idea, they should use it as the repetitive image in a longer poem. Teachers should remind students to experiment with line breaks and word placement. Students may also want to have their repetitive line symbolic in its imagery, adding depth to the meaning of their poem.

2. The idea of layering images, altering their form, and repeating the original and altered images is a medium that adapts itself well to the visual arts. Using the model above, students should create a single image of a theme of their choice. Through the use of layering, repetition, and alteration, the students should produce a visual representation of their idea. This project could use collage, computer imagery, photocopying, or sculpture.

3. In order to understand fully the form of a fugue, students should listen to several musical selections of this style of composition. Teachers should identify the main theme or melody and students can listen for the repetitions and development of new elements in the composition.

**Poetry**

## Shema

You who live secure
In your warm houses,
Who return in the evening to find
Hot food and friendly faces:

Consider whether this is man,
Who labors in the mud
Who knows no peace
Who fights for a crust of bread
Who dies at a yes or a no.
Consider whether this is a woman
Without hair or name
With no more strength to remember
Eyes empty and womb cold
As a frog in winter.

Consider that this has been:
I commend these words to you,
Engrave them on your hearts
When you are in your house, when you walk on your way,
When you go to bed, when you rise.
Repeat them to your children.
Or may your house crumble,
Disease tender you powerless,
Your offspring avert their faces from you.[3]

—Primo Levi

**Shema — Primo Levi**

### Analysis of "Shema"

It is important for students to understand the origins of the title "Shema" in order to appreciate fully the power of Levi's language. The *Shema* is an ancient Hebrew prayer recited by Jews all over the world. Its origins are from the Torah, the Five Books of Moses. The prayer declares the sovereignty of the Divine One and is to be recited daily at dawn and sundown. The prayer should be the first words man and woman utter upon rising and the last words said before sleep. The literal translation of the prayer is: "Hear O Israel: The Lord is our God, the Lord is One."[4] The body of the text of the prayer is as follows:

You shall love Hashem, your God, with all your heart and soul and with all your resources. Let these matters that I command you today be upon your heart. Teach them to your children and speak of them when you sit in your home, while you walk on your way, when you retire and when you arise. Bind them as a sign upon your arm . . . and between your eyes. And write them on the doorposts of your house and your gates. [5]

The words of this prayer are steeped in Jewish tradition and symbol. With the commands for love and obedience, the foundation of the Jewish religion is exemplified. The importance of the legacy of these commandments to future generations is explicit, and the Shema is the first prayer taught to young children of the Jewish faith. Recitation of this prayer exhibits complete devotion and insures peace of mind and God's acceptance of your prayers. The directive to mark the doorposts became the *mezuzah*. This is a small encasement placed on the doorposts of Jewish homes with the prayer Shema written on parchment within it. Jews acknowledge the presence and power of God when entering and leaving a home by touching the mezuzah and kissing their fingertips.

Delivering its message in startlingly commanding tones, the prayer is written in the imperative verb tense. The final paragraph of the prayer declares observance of this prayer will result in days of abundant rains and harvest, but those choosing to ignore God's command will find the "wrath of God will blaze against you." [6] These symbols become the body of the images in Levi's poem and add greatly to its message.

Primo Levi adopts the voice of this prayer in his poem "Shema." The imperative verb tense comes directly from the Ten Commandments of the Old Testament. The first stanza of the poem begins in an accusatory tone with the use of the collective "you" as the author singles out those who enjoy the comforts of life, "Hot food and friendly faces" (l.4). Levi ridicules the complacency and comfort. In the next stanza, he gives an opposite view to reinforce the comfort of these people. Using the voice of the original Shema, Levi admonishes these people to "Consider" the plight of the victims of the Holocaust. The implication of using the word "consider" is intense. Levi wants the world to make this command one that is given serious and committed discussion and remembrance. The second stanza delivers this command in poignant but minimal language in the description of the men and women who must fight for survival, as opposed to the images of the satisfied in the first stanza. This simple second stanza reveals the suffering of the starving, the shamed, and the barren, lost ones who were victims of the Nazis.

The final stanza is most eloquent in its tone of benediction. In similar language to the prayer Shema, Levi again commands the people to "Consider" what has been. The use of the imperative verbs "Consider," "Engrave," and "Repeat" is astounding in its impact. This command from a higher power must be observed. The word "engrave" symbolizes the mezuzah, and Levi replaces this Shema with his own: a commandment to remember and honor the victims of the Holocaust. Similar to the original prayer, Levi ends his poem with a powerful curse, "Repeat them to your children. /Or may your house crumble, /Disease tender you powerless, /Your offspring avert their faces from you" (l.20–23). The curse of being rejected by your offspring is the ultimate threat. The prospect of being rejected and abhorred by your children defies one of the basic tenets of Judaism: the importance of family and honor to your parents.

An interesting question to ask students is about the voice of the narrator. To whom is he addressing these remarks? Are they the men and women who perpetrated these horrors upon the Jewish people, or are they the Jews themselves? If in fact Levi is commanding the Jews to remember, there is an important difference in the tone of the poem. He poses the commands to survivors and other Jews who may have buried their memories of the concentration camps in the "goodness" of their present lives. The call of the Shema becomes the call to Kaddish, the prayer of mourning for the dead.

## Writing Ideas

The tone of this poem is an interesting one with which students can identify. Students could be encouraged to write their own poems in an imperative voice. The writing exercise could begin with a list of imperatives. What do students see as the most important issues in their lives? Teachers could begin with the following prompts:

1. What contemporary issues of life do you feel most compelled to support? To protest?
2. To what are you absolutely willing to commit yourself on a daily basis in order to help your community?
3. What should children never forget?
4. What should adults never forget?

Responses to these questions could be written in prose, then converted to poetry.

### Landscape

Tall poplars—human beings of this earth!
Black ponds of happiness—you mirror them to death!
I saw you, sister, stand in that effulgence.[7]

—Paul Celan

## Landscape — Paul Celan

### Analysis of "Landscape"

The poem "Landscape" is written in a minimalist style. Minimalism is the reduction of idea or feeling to its barest, most essential parts. It is the use of specific language and its placement in the text that creates the poem's impact, not extensive detail, metaphor, or imagery.

"Landscape" is written as a tribute to "The tall poplars—human beings of the earth" (l.1). Students could read the poem with the insertion of the word "like" to help in understanding this simple metaphor: "Tall poplars— [like] human beings of the earth." The comparison of a human being to a poplar is strong and simple in its message. The poplar is an erect and stately tree that grows to great heights, usually in a grove of like trees. Celan follows this metaphor with the paradoxical labeling of ponds as "Black ponds of happiness—you mirror them to death" (l.2). This is an opposing image of beautiful ponds blackened by the horror of what they witness—the death that surrounds them. The poplars/humans proudly but despairingly give witness to the atrocities of the camps while mirroring their own fate of death.

The last line of this poem becomes a more personal tribute with the use of the word "sister" (l.3). "Sister" can be interpreted as a blood relation or it can represent the sisterhood of those who died in the death camps. The sisters stand in the "effulgence," the radiating light of the poplars. They stand erect with the other victims of the Holocaust, proud and enduring in their memory.

This poem is written as an ode to the victims of the Holocaust. An ode is tribute to a much beloved or respected idea or image. Odes are often tributes to an object of beauty, a season, an image of nature, or a person. Odes can be written in the simplest of language embellished with symbols and detailed description. The reading of this form of poetry is helpful to students, and the authors William Carlos Williams, e. e. cummings, William Wordsworth, and Shakespeare all provide examples of this artistic form.

### Writing Ideas

1. Students should compose several odes of their own. Emphasis on tone is important in this exercise, as an ode is often a hyperbole of expressed emotion and love.
2. Science teachers can also use this form of poetry to extol the virtues of a scientific phenomenon such as earthquakes, tornadoes, falling stars, rainbows, chemical reactions, or any natural aspects of the planets.
3. The recitation of odes is a wonderful opportunity to explore voice and performance. Students should create tableaux of their odes, using memorization and performance to showcase their poetry.

Poetry

Poetry

### Chorus of the Orphans

We orphans
We lament to the world:
Our branch has been cut down
And thrown in the fire—
Kindling was made of our protectors—
We orphans lie stretched out on the fields of loneliness.
We orphans
We lament to the world:
At night our parents play hide and seek—
From behind the black folds of night
Their faces gaze at us;
Their mouths speak:
Kindling we were in a woodcutter's hand—
But our eyes have become angel eyes
And regard you,
Through the black folds of night
They penetrate—
We orphans
We lament to the world:
Stones have become our playthings,
Stones have faces, father and mother faces
They will not wilt like flowers, nor bite like beasts—
And burn not like tinder when tossed into the oven—
We orphans we lament to the world:[8]

—Nelly Sachs

## Chorus of the Orphans — Nelly Sachs

The title of this poem, "Chorus of the Orphans," is significant to the understanding of it. A chorus is a joining together of voices to repeat an echoing refrain. In Greek tragedy, the chorus was used as the voice of conscience and pathos, the voice that expressed emotion and public reaction to events and ideas. Nelly Sachs uses this image of chanting and judgment to express the voices of the orphans, the children left behind, bereft of their parents because of the Holocaust. These voices of the orphans join together to deliver the message of this poem in a moving tribute to their strength and hope.

The use of metaphor is the supporting form of this poem. Sachs creates the metaphor of a tree to paint the images of both the children and their parents. The children "lament" (l.2) the cutting of their branches. The use of the word lament implies mourning and suffering. The children mourn the shearing of these branches that represent their limbs reaching out for protection and an embrace from their "protectors" (l.5). The limbs of the tree are the bearers of new growth—the flowering of the leaves and fruit of a tree. The limbs have been amputated, "thrown into the fire" (l.4) of the crematoria, truncating their lives and future. Sachs gives voice to these children using their language and symbols of their games. The childhood game of hide and seek becomes a gruesome search for their parents in the "black folds of night" (l.10). The adventure of a game played in the dark becomes the horror of loss and abandonment, a game where there is no "home free" or safe tree where the children can go to save themselves from capture.

The voices that call these children are not the "all ye, all ye, in free" of hide and seek, but the voices of their lost parents. Sachs changes the voice of the narrator and speaks of the fate of the parents. The image of trees again repeats itself as the "woodcutters," the Nazis, cut down completely the lives of the parents who then become protectors in death, or "angel eyes" (l.14) who penetrate the blackness of night.

In the final lines of the poem, the children again join voices as they describe, "Stones have become our playthings./Stones have faces, father and mother faces" (l.21). Stones are the gravestones, the markers of their parents, carved with the faces of their parents, permanent, unable to burn. The permanence of memory is a powerful image here, stones as indestructible, not vulnerable like the trees.

The poem's last line is a fragment, the repeating of the voices, with a colon as its end mark. This colon is significant in its lack of conclusion. The chorus of voices will forever remain and the colon prepares the reader for a continuing lament, one that has no end.

Nelly Sachs also wrote a poem entitled "Chorus of the Rescued."[9] This poem follows the same pattern and style as "Chorus of the Orphans," continuing beyond the colon at the end of "Chorus of the Orphans." The "Chorus of the Rescued" again uses the voice of the children detailing their lives after their "rescue" from abandonment. Interesting discussion happens when students study these poems in comparison to each other.

**Poetry**

### Writing Ideas

1. The style of this poem is an extended metaphor. Students could make a list of the five most significant events of their lives to date. Choosing one, they should write another list of all the images that best define this important moment. After completing this list, students should "translate" these images into metaphor, choosing one predominant idea or image as the method of comparison. For example, crossing the street unaccompanied by an adult for the first time could be compared to accomplishing a challenge in their lives today. These poems can also use repetition as a means to emphasize their voice.

2. Because of the use of refrain in Holocaust poetry, students could work collaboratively to put the lines of this poem to music. They could compose music of their own, or choose a composition that parallels the emotion and impact of the poem. Performance of these pieces could be a class project.

**Written in Pencil in a Sealed Railway Car**

Here in this carload
I am eve
With abel my son
if you see my other son
cain of man
tell him that i [10]

—Dan Pagis

**Written in Pencil in a Sealed Railway Car — Dan Pagis**

### Analysis of "Written in Pencil in a Sealed Railway Car"

This poem by Dan Pagis is based upon the biblical story of Cain and Abel. Reading the second chapter of Genesis in the Old Testament would help students to understand the reference. Pagis uses the characters Cain and Abel, two rivaling brothers, to represent the Jews and the Nazis. Abel becomes the victim and Cain the symbol of evil.

The narrator's voice of this poem is the mother of "cain" and "abel" (l.3, 5). As "eve," the matriarch of all generations of humankind, her plea embodies compassion for her son "abel" and discordant loss of her son "cain." With the message to "cain" left unstated or cut off by the image of complete despair or death, Pagis implies that understanding or forgiveness for the Cains of the world is unutterable, indefinable, without words.

This poem is often printed in cursive type to create the effect of authentic handwriting. It is important for students to understand that this is a poetic representation of emotion, not an actual document from the death trains of the Holocaust.

### Writing Ideas

1. Archetypal and legendary characters are often used in poetry to represent an emotion or event. Students could brainstorm together a list of memorable figures in history or mythology. What do each of them represent? What are the myths that they embody? Students might then choose one legendary character and write a poem that uses her/him as the theme of their writing. For example: How do the actions and words of Martin Luther King Jr. embody courage and honor? What qualities does Abraham Lincoln represent that are relevant to our lives today?

2. Students could choose individuals from their own lives who have greatly influenced them and write an ode in honor of him or her.

### I, The Survivor

I know of course; it's simply luck
That I've survived so many friends. But last
night in a dream
I heard those friends say of me: "Survival of
the fittest"
And I hated myself.[11]

—Bertolt Brecht

## I, The Survivor — Bertolt Brecht

### Analysis of "I, The Survivor"

The poem "I, The Survivor" was written by Bertolt Brecht in an attempt to give voice to the countless numbers who escaped the Nazis and survived. The poem expresses the burden of those who did not suffer the pain or death of the concentration camps. It is the voice of the survivor suffering the guilt of not perishing in the Holocaust.

Brecht uses minimal and nondecorative language to express the poem's complex emotion. The use of the word *survivor* comes not as a tribulation or celebratory announcement, but as a shameful declaration of living. Survivors then become not necessarily the victors, but the ones left behind, alone. Brecht declares "it's simply luck/That I've survived so many friends"(1.1–2), not divine privilege or earned freedom.

The image of the dream is powerful. Survivors have the privilege to sleep and dream, but this dream is fraught with meaning and accusation. The lines "Survival of/the fittest" (1.4–5) echo the Nazis' credo of the Aryan race as the fittest. Brecht uses this line in a mocking tone of the dead chiding the survivors.

The last line of the poem gives voice to the disturbing idea of survivors continuing to suffer and live in self-reproachment. Life is now not a gift but a sorrow. Acknowledgement of this emotion is crucial to understanding the lives of those who survived the Holocaust.

After his reluctant immigration to the United States during the war, Brecht returned to Germany in 1949 for the remainder of his life. It would be interesting for students to read additional poetry written after the war for its expression of emotion about the events of the Holocaust.

(See other poetry selections for writing ideas in the minimalist form.)

Poetry

## Suggested Reading

*And the World Stood Silent: Sephardic Poetry of the Holocaust.* Translated by Isaac Jack Levi. Urbana: University of Illinois Press, 2000.

Kovner, Abba. *A Canopy in the Desert: Selected Poems by Abba Kovner.* Shirley Kaufman, ed. Pittsburgh: University of Pittsburgh Press, 1973.

Schiff, Hilda, ed. *Holocaust Poetry.* New York: St. Martin's Press, 1995.

Striar, Marguerite M., ed. *Beyond Lament: Poets of the World Bearing Witness to the Holocaust.* Chicago: Northwestern University Press, 1998.

[1] *The New Lexicon: Webster's Encyclopedic Dictionary of the English Language.* Bernard Cayne and Doris E. Lechner, eds. (New York: Lexicon Publications, 1989), p. 383.

[2] Paul Celan, "Death Fugue." *Poems of Paul Celan*, Translated by Michael Hamburger. (New York: Persea Books, 1972), p. 61.

[3] Primo Levi, "Shema," *Against Forgetting*, Carolyn Forché, ed. Translated by Michael Roloff (New York: W. W. Norton & Co., 1993), p. 375.

[4] *Siddur Ahavas Shalom/The Complete Artscroll Siddur* (New York: Mesorah Publications, 1984), p. 91.

[5] Ibid., p. 93.

[6] Ibid.

[7] Paul Celan, "Landscape," *Poems of Paul Celan.* Translated by Michael Hamburger. (New York: Persea Books, 1972,) p. 73.

[8] Nelly Sachs, "Chorus of the Orphans," *O The Chimneys*, Translated by Michael Hamburger (New York: Farrar, Strauss and Giroux, 1967), p. 29.

[9] Ibid.

[10] Dan Pagis, "Written in Pencil in a Sealed Railway Car," *Against Forgetting. Twentieth-Century Poetry of Witness*, p. 387.

[11] Bertolt Brecht, "I, The Survivor," *Images of the Holocaust: A Literature Anthology.* Jean E. Brown, Elaine Stephens, and Janet Rubin, eds. (Lincolnwood, Illinois: NTC Publishing Group, 1996), p. 336.

Poetry

# Art: Before, During, and After World War II ——————

## Introduction

> [Holocaust] . . . art served three functions. It provided a powerful link to a former identity. It was a bridge to the future—one of the few means available to convey the suffering to those who came after it; it was a way to transcend the present by transforming the victim's experience into art.[1]

The study of sculpture, painting, drawing, graphic design, and photography before and during World War II provides an important tool for students to gain a detailed and focused understanding of the Holocaust. Along with the historical documentation of the war, the arts provide additional perspectives on the symbols and images of war. Art prior to the war was a beautiful catalog of life in the villages and towns of Eastern Europe. Art for the victims of the Holocaust was a means of expression that embodied a richness of emotion and judgment and allowed a voice of resistance to be heard. Students can grasp the concepts of art, giving their study of the Holocaust both a written and visual language.

### Objectives for Teaching Art of the Holocaust

Teaching about the art world that existed around the time of the war is an important way for teachers to respond to the many ways students learn through the written word and the visual arts. Art stimulates the imagination and allows new methods of understanding parallel information provided through literature and film. The following are objectives for teaching art of the Holocaust:

- ►To give a visual time line of the history of art before, during, and after the war years
- ►To provide the language of art appreciation
- ►To teach the techniques of viewing a piece of visual art
- ►To interpret symbol and imagery in visual form

### Modern Jewish Art in Russia

Jewish art can best be defined as art that helped "to affirm a distinct cultural identity."[2] The art of the Pale of Settlement in Russia represented the lives of more than five million Jews living there prior to World War I. The Pale was a wide region of Russia stretching from the Baltic to the Black Sea, comprised of little towns and villages that held the majority of the population for this area. The Jews of these towns developed their own religious traditions, government, educational systems, and a strong Yiddish identification through literature, theater, and art.

In the late nineteenth century, Russian art was predominantly neoclassical and nationalistic. The images that dominated the visual arts were based on the Russian Orthodox Church and its iconography. The art of the time was largely realistic in its representation of Russian life. It was a national art that represented the country of Russia and not the distinct cultural differences in its population.

At the turn of the century, a group of young artists emerged from the Pale encouraged by the increasing secularism and enlightenment of Jews in Russia. The dominant nationalistic mood was replaced with an ever-increasing influence from the West. Yiddish theater was dominant at this time as well as the literature that became the voice of the many Jews populating Russia. With the advent of the Russian Revolution, Jewish artists searched for a cultural and political autonomy that represented the millions of Jews of the Russian population. The art of these young men was largely comprised of the folk sources of Jewish traditional life. Steeped in this Jewish cultural heritage, the art came from the uniquely illustrated religious documents and manuscripts, the carvings on gravestones, the architecture of the synagogues, and the beauty of the religious objects used in prayer.[3]

One of the most prominent members of this group of artists was Mark Zakharovish Shagal, known today as Marc Chagall. Chagall was born in Vitebsk, Belorussia, in 1887. His father was a factory worker, and Chagall received his early teaching from his grandfather, who instilled in him a love of the Torah (the Five Books of Moses) and Jewish tradition. At the age of nine, Chagall left the Jewish elementary school he attended to enroll in the Yehuda Pen School of Painting in Vitebsk. From there Chagall continued his studies in St. Petersburg at the school of the Society for the Encouragement of the Arts. In 1910, with increased influences from the West on the artists of Russia, Chagall traveled to Paris where the trend of the Cubist movement transformed his artist's vision for the remainder of his life. In 1914 Chagall returned to Russia where he painted, exhibited, and taught. Chagall collaborated with the Kamerni State Jewish Theater in Moscow redesigning and redecorating this theater with large murals and wall panels between the windows.

Political changes resulting from the Russian Revolution began to impinge on the creativity of the artistic vision of the Jewish artists. The registering of artists and the predominant insistence on "communal art" that represented the cultural and political ideas of Russia discouraged the independence of the Jewish artists. Chagall shared the opinion of other artists that the "most essential qualities of an artist cannot be put into the service of communal institutions."[4] Chagall was frustrated as art in the 1920s became more propagandist in subject matter and was controlled by the state. Social realism dominated the art world, and Chagall left Russia to visit Palestine, Holland, Spain, Poland, and Italy. Because of the increasing persecution of the Jews in Germany and Poland, Chagall left Germany in 1941 to seek shelter in the United States. His departure was one day before the German invasion of Russia. The destruction of the Jewish villages in Russia and Eastern Europe deeply disturbed Chagall, and his paintings reflected the burning streets and murdered Jews. The emphasis of the suffering of the world emerged in his art as Chagall realized he would never return to the Russia of his youth.

Upon his return to France after the war, Chagall had countless exhibits in the West but was largely ignored and shunned in Russia. It was not until 1968 that a small show of Chagall's private paintings was exhibited in Novgorod. Finally in 1987 a large collection of Chagall's work was exhibited in the Pushkin Museum in Moscow, and a Chagall Museum was opened in Vitebsk.

## The Art of Marc Chagall

Chagall best represents the folklorist qualities of the Jewish artists of the Pale of Settlement in Russia. His artistic representation is largely metaphoric, relying on color and characterization of subject to create a poetic vision of his world. Although his art has been labeled as "pictoral," it is the richness of his imagery and representative meanings that separates it from illustrative art. "For him, painting is the illustration of the inner world of images."[5] His paintings are metaphoric representations of the innocent elements of nature, imagination, fairy tales, and folklore, all richly painted with flowers, landscapes, animals, and lovers. His images suggest much more than their illustrations depict and are an assembly of the images of his childhood, religious iconography of the Jewish tradition, and the physical landscape of his home in Vitebsk. The Jewish fiddler, the rabbi, the churches and synagogues, the observations of birth, life, and death all take on mystical qualities with their record of the laughter and tears of festive and solemn occasions in the town of Vitebsk. Legend dominates his imagery and the Divine is represented in his urban landscapes. His post-World War II work reflects the deep human suffering of the Jews in Eastern Europe.[6]

## I and the Village — Marc Chagall — Plate I

(1911. Oil on canvas, 192.1 x 151.4 cm. The Museum of Modern Art, New York. Mrs. Simon Guggenheim Fund. Photograph 2001, The Museum of Modern Art, New York, © 2001 Artists Rights Society [ARS] New York/ADAGP Paris.)[7]

This early painting (see following page) by Chagall refers to the images he used throughout his lifetime to depict the village in which he grew up. Chagall creates a parable that tells the story of life in the Pale of Settlement in Russia. The painting has a multilayered view with characters and images receding and reappearing, superimposed upon each other with a dreamlike quality. There is a feeling of looking through a glass window in which the images are reflected upon each other, giving it a three-dimensional quality. The composition of the painting contains various geometric shapes separated into their own regions but brought together by the central circle. The overall effect is a type of mosaic that is unified by shape and color. Using the dominant colors red, green, and blue with touches of yellow, Chagall creates a clear and radiant picture of a village. Chagall uses this painting to record memory. The tiny village in the background with its domed cathedral, the farmer and his sickle, the maternal cow being milked by a village milkmaid, the innocence of the cow gazing directly into the man's eyes, and the effervescent nosegay in honor of the lamb are all poetic representations of the harmony of this village. Chagall imbues these characters with a dreamlike quality as he places the peasant woman upside down and uses transparent regions to fill space between the shapes. This painting is a collection of symbols that represent memory and a lost time in the Pale of Settlement in Russia.

Art

**I and the Village — Marc Chagall — Plate I**

Art

## White Crucifixion — Marc Chagall — Plate II

(1938. Oil on canvas, 154.3 x 139.5 cm. Gift of Alfred s. Alschuler, 1946.925. Photograph courtesy of The Art Institute of Chicago, © 2001 Artists rights Society [ARS], New York/ADAGP Paris.)[8]

The war years in Eastern Europe invoked new and more solemn pictoral images for Chagall. Troubled by the persecution of the Jews, Chagall began to depict the terror and destruction of the very villages he memorialized in his earlier paintings. This painting, *White Crucifixion*, was a direct response to the news coming out of Nazi Germany. In it Chagall uses the grave image of Christ crucified on the cross, wrapped in a Jewish prayer shawl. The sorrowful face of the Christ figure bears the Hebrew inscription above, "Jesus of Nazareth, King of the Jews."

The Christ figure is lit from above by the raging fire of the synagogue and below by the Jewish menorah (candelabra). Surrounding the crucifixion are images of the war: the man fleeing with the Torah in his arms, the woman clutching a baby, the villagers fleeing in a wooden boat with arms raised in plaintive prayer, the Nazi soldiers overtaking a village and burning the upside-down houses. And flying above in the heavens of this horrific scene are the rabbis, eyes covered, hands extended in frantic supplication and horror. The painting becomes a narrative of the destruction of Jewry in Europe, a powerfully evocative political and human judgment on the devastation wrought by the Nazis.

## Degenerate Art

From 1927–37 the Nazi Party formed the National Socialist Society for German Culture. This censuring group used its power to label art as "Degenerate Art" and launched an exhibition of 650 paintings, sculptures, prints, and books that represented for the Nazis the connection between race and depravity. The works of the exhibit *Entartete Kunst* (Degenerate Art) were displayed in 1937 in Munich and traveled around Germany and Austria for three years. The artists' paintings were exhibited with graffiti and explanatory notes explaining the moral degradation of the artwork. More than three million people viewed this exhibit. Graphic posters advertising the exhibit and declaiming the works of art were exhibited over Germany and Austria. The painters Marc Chagall, Max Beckmann, Paul Klee, and Wassily Kandinsky were exhibited and ridiculed for their post-impressionist and surrealistic style. Much of the work of the artists was abstract in style and condemned by the Nazis for its expressionism. Many of these artists were forced to flee Germany before and during the war.

### Max Beckmann (1884–1950)

Max Beckmann was born in Leipzig, Germany, the child of a successful grain merchant. From a very early age he showed signs of promise as an artist. At the age of sixteen, Beckmann was admitted to the Grandduacal Art School in Weimar. From there, he traveled to Paris and Berlin. The Berlin Secession, a group of progressive artists, made him a member of its executive board in 1910, an honor for such a young man. His early paintings are a reflection of his wartime experiences as a medical corpsman during World War I. The despair and sadness he witnessed characterize these paintings. Although the years of 1924–32 found Beckman painting images of contentment with representations of carnivals and costumed clowns, the impending rise of the Nazi power influenced his work. Labeled as one of the "Degenerate Artists," Beckmann's art was censured, forcing him to leave Germany in 1937. Beckmann lived in Amsterdam in exile, suffering from isolation from his native country. Beckmann eventually moved to the United States in 1947, exhibiting in various large cities and teaching at the Brooklyn Museum Art School in New York in 1950. That same year, he died. Beckmann was the winner of several art prizes during his lifetime including first prize in the Golden Gate International Exposition in San Francisco in 1939 and an honorary doctorate from Washington University.

Eleven of Beckmann's lithographs and etchings, titled *The Berlin Journey*, were exhibited at *Entartete Kunst*. The painting *Christus und die Ehebrecherin* (*Christ and the Woman Taken in Adultery*, Figure 6) depicts Christ forgiving an adulteress. His hand is raised in defiance of the guards at the gate ready to remove the woman. A figure to the right of the painting points his finger in ridicule at the "fallen" woman while a man to the left mourns her inevitable capture. The National Socialists deemed this painting an affront to the values of marriage and family. Included in the exhibit was the *Kreuzabnahme* (*Deposition*, Figure 164). This painting depicts the crucified Christ being taken down from the cross as the woman below him shields her eyes and is consoled by a young girl. Hitler strongly condemned any religious representations that distorted a view of Christianity. In this painting, the emaciated Christ, barely clad, with an astounded look on his face, affronted the image of Christianity for the Nazis. Various etchings and paintings depicting lovers such as *Liebespaar* (*Lovers*, Figure 170) and *Umarmung* (*Embrace*, Figure 177) were included in this exhibit. The Nazis condemned these paintings as depictions of carnal and amoral acts.[9]

## Paul Klee (1879–1940)

Paul Klee was born in Münchchenbuchseen near Bern, Switzerland. Both his parents were trained musicians and his father held German citizenship, which Paul adopted. As a child, Klee considered a career in music, but was drawn to the art world. In 1899 he was admitted to the Munich Academy where he studied the strict conventional mechanics of art. Inspired by the Renaissance art he viewed on a trip to Italy in 1903, Klee produced a series of etchings in this style. Klee was very much influenced by the impressionists Van Gogh and Cézanne, but also studied the work of the cubists. He became friends with Wassily Kandinsky and began to paint in an abstractionist style. In 1916 Klee was forced to serve in the German army and upon his return from war, his paintings reflected romantic, childlike qualities. It was in 1920 that he joined the teaching staff of the Bauhaus, a school of modern art, where he experimented with the relationship of art to architecture. The Nazis denounced Klee in 1933, and he was condemned in the exhibition *Entartete Kunst*. Klee returned to Switzerland and painted until his death in 1940.

Seventeen works of art by Klee were chosen for *Entartete Kunst*. Klee's abstractions were considered evidence of his "mental derangement," and his art was labeled childlike. The National Socialist's critique of Klee's art was that it was created by a demented individual who suffered from psychological instabilities. The Nazi Party shunned individuals who were considered to have diminished mental abilities, and they labeled Klee's work that of a madman. The lithograph *Die Heilige vom innern Licht* (*The Saint of the Inner Light*, Figure 275) was exhibited with notes that labeled it as the "work of a mental patient," noting its distorted images. His *Twittering Machine* was considered an infantile example of art produced by a mentally ill person.[10]

The censuring of art was extended by the Nazi Party to literature and music, which were also labeled "Degenerate." (See chapters on Music of the Holocaust and *Stones from the River*.)

Art

### Anti-Semitic Art and Propaganda

The Nazis were relentless in their production of anti-Semitic propaganda. They created the National Socialist Racial Policy which outlined the unacceptable physical and intellectual qualities of the Jews of Eastern Europe. With picture books for children and pamphlets and newspapers for adults, the Nazis drew upon the myths of Jews as swarthy, large-nosed men and women who took part in the ritual slaughter of innocent Christian children. The widely read newspaper of Julius Streicher, *Der Sturmer,* denounced Jews as crude and vicious. It used cartoons to depict Jews as "The Scourge of Poland and Germany." Poster art showed Jews as prosperous shopkeepers with starving Germans in the background. Various representations of Germany crucified on the cross with Jews leering in the background were displayed throughout Germany and Austria. Satirical cartoons and essays on emigration, prayer, teachers, and family life flooded the newspapers.

The Nazis also used film to spread propaganda. Hitler contracted the young filmmaker Leni Riefenstahl to produce a film about the 1934 Nuremburg Nazi Party Conference. Titled *Triumph of the Will,* the film documented the thousands of adoring citizens and young, robust German soldiers in Nuremburg greeting Hitler. Hitler's speech was filmed before a crowd of thousands glorifying his denouncement of the Jews. Riefenstahl went on to film the Berlin Olympics in the propagandist documentary *Festival of the Nations, Parts One and Two.* Teachers should consult the website:

www.calvin.edu.academic/cas/faculty/streich3htm

for an extensive reference to the propaganda of Nazi poster art, documents, cartoons, and pamphlets.[11]

### Art of the Holocaust

> Painting is an instrument of war to be waged against brutality and darkness.[12]

The deportations to the concentration and death camps of Eastern Europe included the arrests of countless members of the artistic community. With his vision of the Nazi world, Hitler enforced his definition of what types of art, music, and literature represented the Aryan nation: romantic, nationalistic, and realistic to form. Because of his dictates, artists, graphic designers, cartographers, engineers, and architects lost not only their physical freedom of expression, but also their emotional and creative freedoms to produce personal and autonomous art. What emerged from the death camps was art as documentation of the horror of the Nazi Party. The art produced in the camps was a personal reflection of the world surrounding the artists who recorded a world never before seen by the human eye. Its purpose was rooted in the desire and compulsion of the camp and ghetto inmates to give witness to the atrocities inflicted upon the Jews. Art became the missing language used to represent the terror of camp life. It also allowed inmates to recreate the reality of their past lives and affirm their existence despite the attempts by the Nazis to annihilate their artistic spirit and ability. This art, in its documentary style, is a lasting and permanent record of the atrocities of the camps; its legacy gives physical proof to the events of the Holocaust to be passed down to future generations.

Art

"Art of the Holocaust" should be distinguished from "Holocaust art." Men and women who actually experienced the brutality of the Nazis in the concentration and death camps created the art of the Holocaust. Holocaust art is the art created as a reflection of and reaction to the events of the Holocaust by the generations of artists living during and after the war who did not experience the events directly. In discussing art, this unit will focus on art of the Holocaust from the camps Terezín and Auschwitz-Birkenau.

## Art from Terezín and Auschwitz-Birkenau

The concentration camp Terezín was located in a city in Czechoslovakia. Its original purpose was to serve as a model "ghetto camp," and in November of 1941, the transports began arriving at the gates of this city. Theresienstadt (German translation) was a fortress enclosed by thick walls surrounded by a moat. Within the walls of the town was the "small fortress" known as the *Kleine Festung*. Here the SS set up their offices inside a building that had a prison replete with torture chambers and a shooting gallery. The railroad ran directly through the town making it possible to transport inmates to Auschwitz-Birkenau. Terezín was a collection point for the deportations to Auschwitz-Birkenau.

Terezín was designed to be a model camp where visual and performing artists were located. The "model camp" provided a place to bring visiting dignitaries and entertain them with the operas, concerts, and artwork of the inmates. This camp was depicted as a "cultural center" and place for the relocation and care of the infirm. In 1944 the Red Cross made a visit to the camp to inspect the treatment of the inmates. In preparation for this inspection, the Nazis ordered the inmates to pave and repair the roads; false building fronts were created to depict a civilized town with a post office, courthouse, and shops. The Red Cross was led on a tour of these false fronts on the main street. The living conditions of the camp behind this subterfuge were atrocious. Overcrowding, starvation, beatings, torture, and death were the ways of the camp. When the inspection was completed, a few questions were asked about why the Jewish population was being confined. The Red Cross was offered explanations of "relocation" because of the war.

Recognizing the talent of the artistic community, the Nazis devised a plan to produce art for the Third Reich. This art was designated as "assigned art." For the functionary use of art, the artists were instructed to create propaganda posters and murals. Their assignments ranged from the painting of numbers on inmates' uniforms to the creation of technical drawings. The Nazis were meticulous and fanatical recordkeepers. They demanded the artists draw maps, charts, and building and road designs. Early in the war, the engravings on gravestones became the last images of the Jews as depicted by the artists. The Germans also had the artists produce counterfeit money and documents. Hitler recognized the value of these artists in portraying the spirit of the Third Reich. Countless portraits of the officers, landscapes, and still lifes were assigned. Artists were also ordered to copy masterpieces that had been confiscated from museums and homes in Eastern Europe. The Germans ordered paintings rendered in the realistic and sentimental style of German art. The colors were high and dramatic with the rounded lines and shapes of the romantic period. Pastoral and idyllic settings were portrayed along with the formal portraiture of officers and their families. The irony of the Nazis' acceptance of the Jews' talents seemed to escape them in their pursuit of the ideal art for their Aryan nation.

The real art of the camp was produced secretly. This recording of the daily events and atrocities of life in the camp is the greatest demonstration of the will and resistance of the human spirit. Under conditions that were simply inhuman, the men and women of Terezín and Auschwitz-Birkenau gave voice and vision to their inner emotions with art that evoked the despair and terror of their experiences. To combat the dictates of the Germans, the artists of these camps worked furiously to secretly produce their own art. With clandestine methods, artists produced sketches and drawings with the few free moments they could steal from their captors. What emerged was a volume of art produced under the threat of beatings, disfigurement, and death.

The Nazis provided the most crude and demoralizing "studios" for the artists. Disease and starvation plagued the inmates as they worked in unheated and unventilated buildings. Early in the war, the Germans provided supplies, and inmates could receive packages. Bartering with the guards was used to obtain supplies for the assigned art. But beneath the canvases of the assigned art, hidden in cracks in the floors and walls, taped to the backs of sheets of paper, or slipped between the sheets of a torn newspaper, the true art of these camps was produced. Because materials were not provided, and the artists were accountable for every pencil stub they were given, they created art from the barest of materials. Charcoal from the fires and ovens was readily available, and it was the predominant medium used, along with pencils, pen and ink, paints made from food scraps, watercolors made from clothes dye, and grease from truck and railroad wheels. Tissue paper, newspaper margins, matchbox covers, stamp-sheet margins, wrapping paper, and pieces of paper found on the ground pasted and taped together became the surfaces for the drawings and paintings. Bed linen and potato sacks were also used, along with scraps of wood and boards from the floors. In Auschwitz-Birkenau, the walls were filled with art. In the latrines, on doorposts, under stairwells, on windowsills, on the floors and ceilings, artists left their testimony of their existence. It is difficult to imagine the risk these artists took to document their suffering for the world. Art became a method of expression and documentation, and the fervency with which the artists secretly worked is evident in the quality and quantity of sketches and charcoal drawings produced.

In order to have students examine and reflect on the art of the Holocaust, it is important to give some historical perspective to the art created prior to the war. Expressionism was the predominant artistic style of the time. Emerging from the aftermath of World War I, this art is characterized by its intensity of emotion. Bold colors and energetic lines and shapes comprised the forms of the compositions. The anxieties and feelings of the time were portrayed with a new vision, and art became the social criticism of the times. The painting of abstract art in a surrealistic style was also evident in this art period. Surrealism worked to reveal the unconscious, to move beyond reality and day-to-day perceptions of the world. It would be interesting for students to study the art of Pablo Picasso, Marc Chagall, Käthe Kollwitz, and Max Beckmann, the artists of this time. The artists of the Holocaust studied these artists and were aware of their styles. How then did the artists of the Holocaust utilize a visual language to document, interpret, and express this unique event in history?

The art of the Holocaust distinguishes itself with new archetypes of symbols and images that depict suffering and death. Predominant images used by the artists were of the death wagons. These elaborately painted and decorated hearses were confiscated from the ghettos of Poland and Czechoslovakia and used in mockery of the Jewish people. The wagons would draw behind them carts filled with bodies, the procession devoid of dignity and religious ritual. These hearses became the symbol of the degradation of death at the hands of the Nazis. They were depicted in countless ways in the drawings and paintings. Other symbols used were barren trees with limbs like empty arms reaching out, spindly and fragile. The bleakness of the charcoal drawing becomes evident by the medium used and the characterization of the figures in the drawings. Empty eyes, sunken faces, and skeletal postures were drawn with dismal and hopeless landscapes. The drawings were a symbol of "the slow dissolution of the human form" and the blurring of images and lack of distinct features supported this symbol. Barbed wire, food lines, labor detail, burial pits, and roll call were also repeated images in the art. The largeness of the enemy in comparison to the tortured was exemplified in many of the sketches. Empty soup bowls and tearless eyes are also recurring symbols of the art of the Holocaust.

In the death camp Majdanek, artists were allowed to set up sculptures within the compounds. Their designs and installations secretly represented acts of resistance to the prisoners. These acts of protest were significant to the morale of the prisoners. The pieces of sculpture had symbolic meaning in the images they portrayed. In May 1943 a prisoner named Albin Maria Boniecki designed and constructed a sculpture titled *Column of the Three Eagles* (see page 149), where ashes of murdered prisoners were secretly buried beneath the base. A sculpted turtle placed at the exit of Compound 3 was a call for prisoners to slow down on the production lines in the forced-labor factories. Some prisoners associated the turtle with the SS men, reptilian in intellect and demeanor.[13]

## Bedrich Fritta, 1907–44

Bedrich Fritta was a Czech painter born in 1907 in Moravia. He was primarily an illustrator for the periodical *Simplic*. In 1941 Fritta was deported to Terezín with his wife and three-year-old son Tomás. There he directed the Technical Office and worked in secret on a children's alphabet book and numerous sketches. Fritta was a tireless supporter of the artists of Terezín. He recorded with terrifying accuracy the deplorable conditions of the camps. Following the Red Cross visit in 1944, Fritta, along with Leo Haas, was accused of smuggling drawings out of the camp. These drawings showed the inhumane treatment of the Jews in Terezín by the Nazis. Both Haas and Fritta were arrested during what was to be called the Painters Affair of 1944 and detained in the "small fortress" of Terezín. There they were both severely beaten and suffered terribly at the hands of their interrogators. It was reported that Haas carried the gravely ill Fritta on his back to the deportation trains for Auschwitz-Birkenau where Fritta later died from his injuries and the deplorable conditions of the camp.

Art

**Lodging in the Attic — Bedrich Fritta — Plate III**

(Ink wash, 15 x 11 in. Copyright permission granted by Thomas Fritta Haas.)[14]

This sketch depicts the overcrowded barracks in a building at Terezín. The perspective of the sketch is from the narrow background to the more open foreground. This tunnel effect with its wooden floorboards and ceilings suggests the image of a coffin. The light comes from the single window in the background, a symbol of the freedom of the "outside world." The movement of the sketch with its characters eating, talking, sleeping, and bathing is in stark contrast to the skeletal paralysis of the man in the foreground. With hollowed cheeks and empty eyes, he stares helplessly, with little expression.

Art

## Leo Haas 1901–83

Leo Haas was born to a Jewish family in Opava, Moravia, and began to study art at a very young age. In 1919 he attended the Karlsruhe Art Academy, and in 1922 he moved to Berlin where he remained until 1924. The expressionists Goya and Toulouse-Lautrec influenced him. He worked as an illustrator for *Stunde*, a German magazine, and published drawings and several books of illustrations before the war. Haas returned to Czechoslovakia in 1926 and painted there until 1938, traveling frequently to Southern France. Haas was a member of the Moravian and Czech artists' associations, and he worked to have at least one Czech painter at every German exhibit. The Germans labeled him a "cultural Bolshevik," and he was arrested in 1939 for aiding illegal emigration across the German border. Haas was deported to Nisko, near Lublin, then to Ostrava where he worked in forced labor details. In 1942 he was deported to Terezín where he hid his illegal drawings in the wood and plaster walls. He was arrested and placed in the "Small Fortress" of Terezín for smuggling art out of the camp, and then was transferred to Auschwitz and then Sachsenhausen. While in Terezín, Haas became close to Bedrich Fritta and his young son Tomás. Haas dedicated himself to Fritta, carrying him on his back to the trains for deportation to Auschwitz where Fritta died. Later, when Haas was deported to Mauthausen, he took Fritta's son Tomás with him, and upon their liberation from the camp, Haas raised him as his child after the war.

When Haas returned to Czechoslovakia after the war, he retrieved over four hundred of his drawings and sketches of camp life and donated them to the Terezín Memorial and the State Jewish Museum in Prague. Until 1955 Haas worked as a political caricaturist of the Czech party and eventually moved in 1955 to East Germany where he continued to paint his memories of the camps until his death in 1983.

## Mortuary — Leo Haas — Plate IV

(1943. Ink wash, 13-1/2 x 8 in. Copyright © Artists Rights Society [ARS], New York/VG Bildkunst, Bonn.) [15]

This ink wash (on the following page) by Haas captures the inhumanity of the conditions in Terezín. Haas draws the lifeless form of a body upon a crude wooden pallet, barely covered with an inadequate piece of cloth. The perspective of the sketch forces the reader to see the emerging feet and emaciated legs tied down by rope, representing the disrespect for the human being that died. The only other physical feature that documents the humanity of this corpse is the uncovered hands. The pail and sponges for washing the body symbolize the importance and sanctity in Jewish tradition of preparing a body for burial. A small scrap of paper in the right corner has the name of the dead scribbled illegibly.

Art

Art

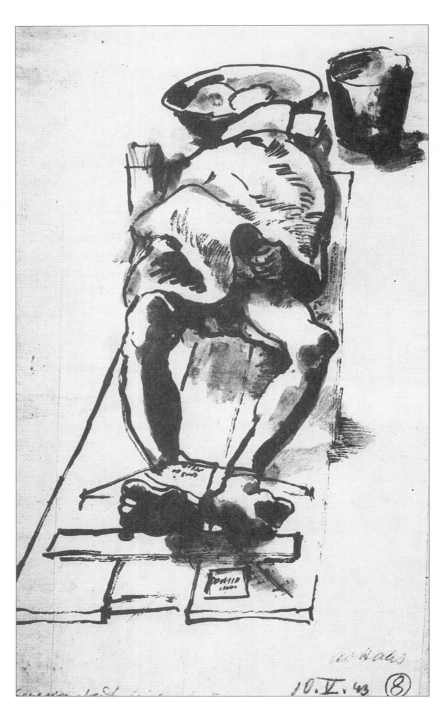

**Mortuary — Leo Haas — Plate IV**

## Hunger — Leo Haas — Plate V

(1943. Ink wash, 18 x 24 in. Copyright © 2001 Artists Rights Society [ARS], New York/VG Bild-Kunst, Bonn.)[16]

This drawing by Haas depicts the desperation of the inmates of Terezín. The drawing is a panoply of emaciated faces with sunken features, people clothed in rags, hands clutching empty bowls, arms outstretched in supplication for food. They emerge from under a crumbling wall of bricks, crowding and pushing their way toward emptiness. The line of the begging men and women stretches far into the background of the drawing emphasizing the numbers of nameless prisoners in the camp. The blackened Star of David is affixed on the coat of one of the figures and stands out in this sea of unknown human beings. In the foreground, the people appear to be standing in a bottomless pool of water that has floating in it a wooden box of skeletal pieces. A barely recognizable skeleton emerges from this box, its bony fingers clutching the empty dipper. The hopelessness and despair pictured on the faces of these figures depicts the horror of life and death in the camp Terezín.

Art

## Holocaust Memorials

Countless works of art have been created throughout Europe, Israel, and the United States memorializing those who lost their lives and those who resisted during the Holocaust. Museums have been built, sculptures dedicated, and paintings created all in the spirit of remembrance. Many of these works of art can be found at the former concentration and death camps in Eastern Europe. Sculptured works have been commissioned to create art that represents the horror, fear, courage, and triumphs of the human spirit. Memorials have been erected that represent the lives lost from many different nationalities as well as those who resisted Fascism. Students should research the political implications of the commission of these sculptures and the conflicts between the German government, private citizens, and survivor groups. Students should look at the post-war Communist domination and manipulation of the concentration-camp sites and commissioned memorials. (See Art from Terezín and Auschwitz-Birkenau.) The struggle between letting history record the events of the war versus the pledge to "Never Forget" is represented in the ongoing creation of artwork in memory of the Holocaust.

The following is a brief discussion of several of the memorial sites at the camps Majdanek, Dachau, and Auschwitz-Birkenau in memory of the victims of the Nazis. Teachers and students should consult the web site:

http://fcit.coedu.usf.edu/Holocaust/RESOURCE/Gallery/gallery5.htm

for photographs and a video of the camp memorials. (See Suggested Reading for book sources.)

## Majdanek

The contemporary memorial at Majdanek, designed by Wiktor Tolkin, is comprised of two parts. The first is an enormous, abstract sculpture that appears to sit precariously on two stone columns. The appearance of the sculpture is one of foreboding and danger, as it appears that it will topple over at any moment. This is representative of the past and possible future dangers. Steep steps leading under the sculpture are symbolic of the experience of entering the underground gas chambers. The second part of the memorial, the mausoleum, is approached along the "black road" or "road to hell" which housed the bathhouses and gas chambers. As you approach the mausoleum, the *Column of Three Eagles* is on the right. Created by the inmates of the camp, the eagles express the prisoners' desire for freedom. The inmates also hid an urn with ashes of victims in its base. The half-mile route ends at the mausoleum. Before the visitors is a domed structure elevated on three stone pillars, which covers a huge bowl that contains a mound of human ash and bone. An engraved sign reads, "Let our fate be a warning to you." To the right of this dome is the huge chimney of the gas chamber.[18] (See Art of Terezín and Auschwitz-Birkenau.)

## Dachau

The International Monument at Dachau, the first concentration camp built, was designed and sculpted by Glid Nandor, 1927–97. Nandor, the son of Jews murdered in Auschwitz, spent time in forced labor and fought with the Yugoslavian partisans. His design is devoted to the suffering victims of the camps. The sculp-

*Top:* Majdanek's abstract sculpture, sitting precariously on two stone columns. (Robert I. Katz, © 1998)

*Above:* The domed mausoleum at Majdanek containing a mound of human ash and bone. (Robert I Katz, © 2000)

*Right: The Column of Three Eagles,* expressing the prisoner's desire for freedom. (Robert I. Katz, © 2000)

ture resembles the barbed wire used to keep the inmates from escaping the camps. The "wire" is composed of the twisted and elongated skeletal bodies of the inmates stretched tightly between wooden posts. The hands and feet are angled joints in the shape of abstract stars that claw at the wire. The faces of the victims are open-mouthed, screaming in silent cries of terror and anguish. Bold raised lettering on a plaque bears the inscription, "Never Again."[17]

### Auschwitz-Birkenau

The death camp at Auschwitz-Birkenau is a standing monument to the murder of Jews by the Nazis. The railroad gates with the metal insignia *"Arbeit Mach Frei,"* "Work Will Set You Free," lead into the camp. The gas chambers and crematoria have been preserved, as well as displays of the countless shoes, suitcases, Zyclon B canisters, personal objects, and the hair and teeth of the victims. Great strife was experienced over the approval of the memorial at Birkenau, with the Germans objecting to individual's submissions of design. The final design was a collaborative effort and was unveiled in May 1967. Included in the original memorial was a tower of rectangular stones resembling human forms: a mother, father and child. But this monument of figures was never unveiled and was replaced with square stones of polished marble. This row of blocklike, elevated sarcophagi resembles the boxcars that brought the victims to the camps. Originally, the words inscribed on these tablets were, "Four million people suffered and died at the hands of the Nazi murderers between the years of 1940 and 1945." Twenty-three years later, with the change in the German political regime, the communists removed the inscriptions on the stones. Only in recent years has a new inscription replaced the old that reads: "May this place where the Nazis assassinated a million and a half men, women, and children, a majority of them Jews from diverse European countries, be forever for mankind a cry of despair and of warning."

### Teaching Tools

In order to fully understand and interpret a piece of art, it is important for students to have full use of the "language of art." The following is a glossary of terms that provides students with a working vocabulary to study art.

### Glossary of Terms

**Abstract.** An image with no obvious representational visual links; art which distorts the real-life image

**Aesthetic.** A word defining the description of the total art experience including the qualities of beauty, meaning, feeling, thought, and imagination

**Background.** The part of a picture in which the principal figures or objects are shown

**Complementary Colors.** Hues that are opposite on the color wheel

**Composition.** The overall arrangement and organization of visual elements on a two-dimensional surface

**Design.** The aesthetic considerations that guide the overall organization of a work of art

**Expressionism.** Emotion expressed through distortion, exaggeration of color, shape, and surface to maximize emotional impact

**Foreground.** The part of a drawing or painting nearest to the viewer

**Form.** The overall shape and outward appearance of a three-dimensional object

**Hue.** Characteristics of color as defined by their names

**Humanism.** A style of art that depicts the true and realistic emotion of men and women

**Medium.** Materials and surface used to create an art object

**Motion.** The suggestion of movement of characters and images in painting and sculpture

**Non-objective Art.** Drawings, paintings, and sculpture in which no recognizable object appears to the viewer

**Perspective.** The appearance of objects in relationship to each other and in relationship to the foreground, background, and horizon

**Primary Colors.** Those basic hues from which all other hues can be mixed—red, yellow, blue.

**Sketch.** A simple drawing completed quickly

**Space.** The three-dimensional field in which form exists

**Surrealism.** A style of art that emphasizes the unconscious in order to express extreme emotion

**Symbol.** A design element that suggests an idea, image, philosophy, and/or a political or religious belief or feeling

**Texture.** The tactile surface characteristics that can be felt or visually understood

**Value.** Degree of lightness or darkness

Art

## How to View a Piece of Art

The study of art is a multidimensional initiative for teachers and students alike. Art does not exist in a vacuum, but is influenced by the historical and creative past. It is important for students to have at least a beginning understanding of the art movements prior to World War II to give perspective to the inventiveness and creativity that was the foundation for the art of the Holocaust. Students will gain the tools for broadening their perspective of art beyond the initial observation and reaction. Students must ". . . move beyond the physical knowing and into the contextual knowing by making [themselves] aware of the origins, nature, and limits of its historical and cultural setting."[19] Art of the Holocaust is particularly influenced by history and setting, and it is crucial for students to have a knowledge of the events of the Holocaust in order to study the art of this time period.

The following are suggestions for teaching a unit on art. Teachers should stress individual interpretation and a respectful sharing of ideas.

1. Have students sit quietly with an example of art of the Holocaust close beside them or displayed on a slide screen. After taking notes on what they *see* in the artwork, students should write briefly their ideas and feelings about the artwork. They should consider the following questions:
   ▶ What seems familiar to you in the work of art? What is unfamiliar?
   ▶ What feelings are evoked for you in this piece?
   ▶ How does the artist create these feelings?
   ▶ If you could use just one word to describe this piece, what would it be?
2. After this exercise, discussion about the drawing or painting can begin. Encourage students to read what they wrote. Emphasize feeling and reaction.
3. Students should discuss what the single most powerful image of the drawing is. Included in this discussion should be the "whys" and "where."
4. Do the students recognize any symbols in the drawing? How are they depicted?
5. What is the style of the drawing: expressionistic, realistic, abstract, surreal?
6. How does the physical motion of the piece affect the meaning?
   ▶ How does the medium best express meaning?
   ▶ What message did the artist want to convey? Was she/he successful in evoking a reaction, commentary, feeling about the Holocaust?
   ▶ Look at other drawings or paintings by the same artist. How are they similar/different?

## Visual Art Projects and Research Topics

1. Have students make notes on a personal experience of high emotion. Their list should include what colors, sounds, textures, and smells were present. Then, carefully choosing the medium that would best define this emotion, students should create a piece of art that represents this feeling. All mediums should be considered, as well as size, shape, and texture.
2. The symbol of night and blackness is prevalent in Holocaust literature and art. Students should create a piece of art that uses only black and white. Consideration of mood and meaning is important.
3. Students should make a "mood" book. The pages need not be uniform or even made of paper! Each "page" should represent a mood. Consideration of color, texture, and form is important.
4. Bedrich Fritta created an alphabet book for his son Tomás in the camp Terezín. Students should create an ABC book for young children, experimenting with form, color, and characterization. Cartoon drawing and illustration should be considered for this project, too. (See chapter on *Maus*.)
5. Holocaust art has extended itself to sculpture and monument. Students should research the monuments that have been erected and the sculptural art that has been

created to depict the Holocaust. Students could then create their own monument for the Holocaust. This could be completed as a class project, individually, or in small groups.

6. Photography was an important tool used to document life in the villages and ghettos before the Nazi occupation. It was also a documentary tool used by the Nazis and liberators. Students should be encouraged to research the photography of both the Nazis and Jews which gives visual evidence to the atrocities. A unit on photography could include a student project on documentary photography. (See Suggested Reading at end of chapter.)

7. Often art created in the camps was fabricated with "found" objects. "Found art" has a unique texture and form. Students should empty the contents of a desk drawer in their house and create a piece of found art using only the materials of the drawer. Glue and tape can be used as supplemental tools.

8. Students should discuss the representative symbols of modern culture. Selecting an image or symbol of their choice, students should create a drawing or painting that uses this symbol as its predominant image.

9. Students should read and study the art and poetry in *I Never Saw Another Butterfly* (see Suggested Reading). The following are suggestions on how to use the book:

    ▶ Have students look only at the artwork of the children. Choosing one drawing, they should compose their own poem to accompany the art. Students should write their reactions to the drawings: what they see and feel the artist is conveying.

    ▶ Students should read only the poetry of the book and then draw or paint an accompanying picture as an illustration of the poem. Students should consider the symbols and images of the art of the Holocaust.

10. American poster art was dominant during World War II and was used to inspire patriotism and distinguish the Nazis as the enemy. Students should research the history of government-sponsored American propaganda and its effect on the war effort. Students should be encouraged to create a poster of their own that represents a contemporary issue in American life.

11. During the 1950s, the United States was plagued with the threats of Joseph McCarthy and the "Red Scare." Students should research the events of the United States Senate hearings and the resulting censuring of artists, filmmakers, writers, and teachers. Students could also investigate the recent book bannings in this country supported by parents, school boards, and private libraries.

12. Students should research the many Holocaust museums and memorials in the United States, both public and private, to understand the contemporary art in America that remembers the people who were affected by the Holocaust. (See Suggested Reading).

13. The photographer Roman Vishniac traveled throughout Eastern Europe before the war recording the images of Jews in the villages and ghettos. Students should research the photography of Vishniac for a presentation to the class. (See Suggested Reading.)

Art

## Suggested Reading

Barron, Stephanie. Degenerate Art: *The Fate of the Avant-Garde in Nazi Germany*. Los Angeles, California: County Museum of Art, 1991.

Blatter, Janet and Sybil Milton. *Art of the Holocaust*. New York: The Rutledge Press. A Layla Productions Book, 1981.

Brunswick, Barbie Zelizer, ed. *Visual Culture and the Holocaust*. NJ: Rutgers University Press, 2001.

Costanza, Mary. *The Living Witness, Art in the Concentration Camps and Ghettos*. New York: The Free Press. Collier Macmillan Publishers, 1982.

Czarnecki, Joseph. *Last Traces: The Lost Art of Auschwitz*. New York: Atheneum, 1989.

Frayling, Christopher and Helen Frayling. *The Art Pack/a Unique, Three Dimensional Tour through the Creation of Art over the Centuries: What Artists Do, How They Do It, and the Masterpieces They Have Given Us*. Edited by Ron Van Der Mer. New York: Alfred A. Knopf, 1992.

Fritta, Bedrich. *Tommy: To Tommy, for His Third Birthday in Theresienstadt, 11 January 1944*. Yad Vashem, 1999.

Green, Gerald. *The Artists of Terezín*. New York: Hawthorn Books, Inc., 1969.

Haftman, Werner. *Marc Chagall*. Translated by Heinrich Baumann and Alexis Brown. New York: Harry N. Abrams, Inc., Pub., 1973.

Kampf, Avram. *Jewish Experience in the Art of the Twentieth Century*. Massachusetts: Bergin and Garvey Publishers, Inc., 1984.

Langer, Lawrence. *Art from the Ashes: A Holocaust Anthology*. London: Oxford University Press, 1995.

Marzalek, Jósef. *Majdanek, The Concentration Camp in Lublin*. Warsaw: Interpress, 1986.

Vishniac, Roman. *A Vanished World*. New York: Farrar Straus & Giroux, 1983.

_____.*To Give Them Light: The Legacy of Roman Vishniac*. Edited by Marion Wiesel. New York: Simon and Schuster, 1993.

Volavková, Han, ed. *I Never Saw Another Butterfly: Children's Drawings and Poems from Terezín Concentration Camp, 1942–1944*. Expanded second edition by the United States Holocaust Memorial Museum. New York: Schocken Books, 1993.

Art

Young, James E. *The Texture of Memory: Holocaust Memorials and Meaning.* New Haven and London: Yale University Press, 1993.

**Suggested Videos**

*Degenerate Art.* Distributed by PBS Home Video

[1] Janet Blatter and Sybil Milton, *Art of the Holocaust* (New York: The Rutledge Press. A Layla Productions Book, 1981), p. 24.

[2] Avram Kampf, *Jewish Experience in the Art of the Twentieth Century* (Massachusetts: Bergin and Garvey Publishers, Inc., 1984), p. 15.

[3] Ibid., p. 16.

[4] Ibid., p. 44.

[5] Werner Haftman, *Marc Chagall.* Translated by Heinrich Baumann and Alexis Brown (New York: Harry N. Abrams, Inc., Pub., 1973), p. 8.

[6] Ibid., p. 9.

[7] Ibid., p. 54, colorplate 3.

[8] Ibid., p. 91, colorplate 2.

[9] Stephanie Barron, *Degenerate Art: The Fate of the Avant-Garde in Nazi Germany* (Los Angeles, California: County Museum of Art, 1991), pp. 202–09.

[10] Ibid., pp. 279–82.

[11] http://www.calvin.edu.academic/cas/faculty/Streich3 htm.

[12] Mary Costanza, *The Living Witness, Art in the Concentration Camps and Ghettos* (New York: The Free Press. Collier Macmillan Publishers, 1982), p. 19.

[13] Jósef Marzalek, *Majdanek, The Concentration Camp in Lublin* (Warsaw: Interpress, 1986), p. 151.

[14] Blatter, p. 85, figure 99.

[15] Ibid., p. 88, figure 104.

[16] Ibid., pp. 90–91, figure 108.

[17] James, E. Young, *The Texture of Memory: Holocaust Memorials and Meaning* (New Haven and London: Yale University Press, 1993), p. 95.

[18] Ibid., p. 141.

[19] Ibid., p. 124.

**Art**

# MUSIC of the Holocaust ─────────────────────────

## Introduction

> And while the Nazi attitude was, 'Let them have their fun; tomorrow they will no longer exist,' for the culture-thirsty prisoners this was an opportunity for the expression of defiance through artistic means.[1]

Music along with the visual arts provides students with a new way of "seeing" and understanding the events of the Holocaust. This chapter gives a brief summary of the musical genres performed before and during the war and the music created in the concentration camp Terezín.

In its systematic extermination of European Jews, the Holocaust of World War II denied the world the work of thousands of talented musicians. In 1933 the Third Reich established a central office of registration for all musicians in an attempt to control every aspect of cultural life in Germany. This office was named the *Reichsmusikkammer*, and its first president was the composer Richard Strauss. All Jewish musicians were dismissed from their posts and were not allowed to perform in any organized orchestras, chamber-music groups, operas, or choruses. In response to these restrictions, the Jews of Germany created the Cultural Society of German Jews. This group organized private performances and raised money to support musicians. Both the Lodz and the Warsaw ghettos had full orchestras. The ghetto of Vilna had a full liturgical chorus. In eight years, over five hundred musical programs were performed in Germany including operas, chamber-music groups, and full orchestras.[2]

### Objectives for Teaching Music of the Holocaust

The study of music provides an important alternative for study of the Holocaust for students of varying learning styles. Music can be used as a supplemental lesson plan during the study of art and literature of the Holocaust. In integrating music into the Holocaust curriculum, teachers should focus on the following objectives:

- ▶ To understand the role of music composed and performed during World War II
- ▶ To appreciate music as a voice of expression
- ▶ To become familiar with the different genres of music of the Holocaust

## Ghetto Resistance Music

When the Jews of Europe were forced to move into the ghettos, they brought with them their few belongings and their traditions of music and dance. The most prevalent music heard in the ghettos was from the street bands. Organized by Adam Furmanski, these musicians performed traditional music in the cafés, soup kitchens, and streets of the ghettos. Using music that was previously composed, the musicians wrote their own lyrics to reflect the times, a technique called "contra fact." The lyrics were based on the themes of hope, hunger, and revolt. Often accompanying these musicians were dancers and singers. The Internet provides auditory examples of this music, and Klezmer bands perform this genre of music today. (See List of Available Recordings.)

Along with ghetto music, "domestic" music was prevalent in the homes of the Jews of the ghettos.[3] Traditional music and song were part of the religious observances on the holidays, along with the liturgies and prayers of the various holy days.

Out of the street music also came the "resistance" music. Sung by the partisans, these songs were used for inspiration. Hirsch Glik's "Song of the Partisans, Never Say That You Are Trodding the Final Path" became the national anthem for the resistance movement. (See Composers and Their Works, Hirsch Glik.) It was translated into Polish, Hebrew, Russian, Spanish, Romanian, Dutch, and English.[4]

## Degenerate Music

As the Third Reich was gaining power, new music was spreading across Europe. Swinging rhythms and blues made their way across the ocean from the jazz clubs of the United States, and the cafés and cabarets of Germany were filled with people hungry for this new sound. This innovative music of the 1920s and 1930s was labeled as *entartete* or degenerate music. The *Reichmusikkammer* forbade the playing of this music, and many musicians were arrested for their public performances. Along with the jazz of this time, Hitler declared other composers degenerate; the music of Mendelssohn, Mahler, and Schoenberg was banned. Propaganda posters featured grotesque caricatures of African-American musicians. Many American musicians were banned from performing in Germany. Those living there escaped at the start of the war. Musicians who adopted this style of music composed and performed in clandestine venues.

## Music of Terezín

The Germans created Terezín as a "model camp" filled with visual and performing artists. (See Art chapter for a full description of the history of Terezín.) Many musicians were deported to this camp to provide the Germans with a cultural center for the performing arts. Although musical instruments were confiscated as Jews boarded the trains for the various camps, those bound for Terezín were often given leniency, and they kept their instruments. Several stories tell of musicians who dismantled their instruments and hid the various parts amongst their belongings to be

Music

reassembled later. Musicians were released from labor details at Terezín and could practice and compose during the day. The Germans demanded that the music composed and performed be acceptable to the Third Reich, and works of the German masters Beethoven, Wagner, and Schumann were officially performed.

A committee named *Freizeitgestaltung*, or Administration of Free Time, was formed in the camp to organize the activities of the inmates. Educational centers for the children were developed along with the schedules for entertainment and study for adults. In the evenings, the musicians performed their own music, operas, musical theater, and choruses. Often playing in the bitter cold, hungry and suffering from disease, these musicians sustained the spirits of their fellow prisoners. "No opportunity was left unaccounted for in bringing to their fellow inmates a little beauty, diversion, even laughter to make them forget for a fleeting moment the harsh realities of everyday life."[5]

The Germans used these musicians and singers to entertain the Red Cross on an inspection visit of the camp. In the cruelest of uses, the Nazis often had musicians play for the Jews and other prisoners as they descended from the deportation trains and walked to the gas chambers. Musicians performed in small groups. In the death camp Auschwitz-Birkenau, these groups played as prisoners suffered in the interminable *zähl appell*, line-up for roll call.

## Composers and Their Works

This section of the chapter provides a brief profile of the composers Victor Ullman, Hirsch Glick, and Gideon Klein with a list of the works of several of the composers of Terezín. Much like the visual artists of Terezín, the musicians used their art as a form of protest. Music was the voice expressing despair and hope, and the performances for the inmates were moving in their metaphoric messages. Instrumentation became the unheard voice of suffering and provided a temporary escape from the atrocious living conditions of the camps.

### Victor Ullman

Victor Ullman was born in 1898 near the Moravian-Polish border. The son of an Austrian army officer, he was educated in the gymnasium and received private lessons in music. In the early days of his career, he studied in Vienna with the master Schoenberg. In 1927 he was appointed conductor of the New German Theatre and through this opportunity he began to direct choral groups, compose and give private lessons. By 1935 Ullman had completed seven compositions that were performed in Germany. In 1942 Ullman and his family were deported to Terezín where he became a member of the musical committee *Freizeitgestaltung*. While in the camp, Ullman wrote and performed more than twenty compositions for piano, strings, opera, and small orchestras.

The most famous of Ullman's work while in the camp was his composition of *Opera der Kaiser Von Atlantis Oder der Tod Dankt Ab*, *The Emperor of Atlantis* or *Death Abdicated*. This opera was based on the horror of the camps. Hitler was characterized as the Emperor with Goebbels and Göring as the Loudspeaker and Drummer Girl. The theme of the opera was the chaos of war and the horrors of experience for the people of Germany. This was performed with a small orchestra of woodwinds, trumpet, saxophone, piano, banjo, and percussion. Just as the opera was to have its premier, the musicians of Terezín were transferred to Auschwitz-Birkenau and murdered. Ullman also wrote an *Opera of the Children Going to the Gas Chambers* which was performed for the Red Cross inspection visit. (See Jewish Art chapter.) Long after the war, Ullman's manuscript of the *Opera Atlantis* was found and performed in Israel, Germany and the Netherlands.[6]

### Hirsch Glick

Hirsch Glick was born in Vilna in 1920. Escaping a concentration camp in Estonia, Glick joined the partisans. His partisan song "Zog Nicht Kainmo" (Song of the Partisans) was the "national anthem" for the partisans. Glick died while fighting with the underground organizations of Eastern Europe.[7]

### Gideon Klein

Born in Prerov, Czechoslovakia, Gideon Klein distinguished himself as a talented musician in his childhood. Surrounded by the Czech cultural activities of the 1920s, Klein attended the Master School of Prague Conservatory after completing grammar school. There he studied with the masters Ruzena Kurzora and Vilem Kurz. His later studies were cut short by the closing of the universities. In 1941 Klein was deported to Terezín where he worked tirelessly composing and conducting various musical groups. His works include a piano sonata (1943), a string trio (1944), and a madrigal for sopranos, tenor, and bass (1943).

Klein was transferred to Auschwitz-Birkenau in 1943, and then sent to the coal-mining camps in Silesia where he died in 1944. His work continues to be performed throughout the world.[8]

## List of Available Recordings

The following is a list of available recordings of music composed during the Holocaust. It also includes more recent music composed in memory of the events of the Holocaust.

*Chamber Music from Theresienstadt: 1941-45.* Gideon Klein, Victor Ullman. Amsterdam, Netherlands; Englewood, New Jersey. CD. Channel Classics, 1991.

*Hidden History: Songs of the Kovno Ghetto.* CD. United States Holocaust Memorial Museum.

*Rise Up and Fight! Songs of the Jewish Partisans.* CD. USHMM.

*Silenced Voices: Victims of the Holocaust.* CD. Saxonville, MA. Northeastern Records, 1992.

*Terezín: The Music 1941–44.* 2-CD set. Romantic Robot.

## Music As a Reaction to the Holocaust

*A Survivor from Warsaw.* Schoenberg, Arnold. An oratorio of the true story of the uprising in the Warsaw ghetto.

*Dies Irae.* Krzysztof Pederecki. A memorial for the victims of Auschwitz-Birkenau performed at the camp in 1967.

*From the Diary of Anne Frank: Oratio for Voice and Orchestra.* Oskar Morawetz. Uses excerpts from the diary as the text in a tribute to the courage of the Frank family.

*I Never Saw Another Butterfly.* Charles Davidson. A song cycle based on the children's poetry of Terezín.

*Shema, Sargon, Simon.* Musical adaptation of the poem "Shema" by Primo Levi. (See chapter on Poetry.)

*Terezín: Suite for Piano.* Karl Berman. Written for piano performed at Terezín.

### Writing and Presentation Ideas

1. The instruments used in the compositions of the Holocaust represent the different voices of the war: the terror of children and adults, the power and cruelty of the Nazis, the hope for a better future. Students should listen to different selections of music and listen for the individual instrumental voices. Which instruments represent these experiences and emotions? How does the composer use the quality of the instrument as a metaphor to meaning?
2. Choral groups across the world perform contemporary music that honors the events of the Holocaust. Choral students could research the available musical selections and perform a concert for their school.
3. Music has always been used as a means to express political unrest and protest. Students should research the music of the United States from the Revolutionary War to the present time in search of political music. A presentation and discussion of the music for the class could include original compositions by the students.

## Suggested Reading

Fenton, Ruth. *Playing for Time.* Translated from the French by Judith Landry. New York: Atheneum Press, 1977.

*Finding a Voice: Musicians in Terezín. Curriculum Study Guide and CD.* Facing History and Ourselves National Foundation, Inc., 2000.

Karas, Joza. *Music of Terezín: 1941-45.* New York: Beaufort Books, 1985.

Newman, Richard, with Karen Kirtley. *Alma Rosé, Vienna to Auschwitz.* Portland, Oregon: Amadeus Press, 2000.

*Rise Up and Fight: Songs of Jewish Partisans, 1996.* CD. United States Holocaust Memorial Museum.

Rubin, Ruth. *Voices of the People.* New York: McGraw-Hill, 1973.

---

[1] Joza Karas, *Music in Terezín: 1941–1945* (New York: Beaufort Books, 1985), p. 18.

[2] Moshe Hoch, Gila Flam, and Eddie Halpern, "Music of the Holocaust." *Encyclopedia of the Holocaust* (New York: MacMillan Publishing Co., 1990), p. 1022.

[3] www.fcit.coedu.usf.edu/Holocaust/arts/musicVicti.htm,1.

[4] Ibid., p. 2.

[5] Karas, p. 19.

[6] Hoch, p. 1023.

# Supplemental Activities _____

Research, Writing, and Presentation Ideas

1. A timeline that chronicles concurrent historical, political, social, athletic, and artistic events that occurred in other parts of the world during World War II. Break students into groups by time periods and work to collate research for a final presentation.
2. A personal timeline of the student's life chronicling the significant personal and historical events of his/her life to date.
3. Throughout history, there have been camps of incarceration used by warring countries. Students should research the history of these camps and the social and political events that surrounded the formation of these camps. Suggested specific focus: the Boer War, the Japanese-American internment camps in the United States during World War II, the camps in Bosnia, and the ethnic cleansing in Kosovo/Serbia.
4. Issues of man's inhumanity to man are present in the lives of our students daily. Students could research the violence that is prevalent in schools across the United States or U.S. segregation laws. A debate on defining morality as portrayed by the media, literature, art, sports, and religion could define current ethical standards of behavior in our society.
5. Testimonies of survivors that were taken at the liberation of the concentration camps are now being catalogued and published. Students could research these authentic and timely testimonies for an examination of memory and accurate observation.
6. Students should read the Ten Commandments from the Old Testament and debate the significance and importance of this code of moral and ethical behavior.
7. Students could research the history of anti-Semitism in the United States before, during, and after World War II. What impact did this have on the immigration laws and the relocation of survivors in this country?
8. Students could write a Bill of Human Rights defining the necessary and important rights of a child. Students could share individual writings and create an "official document" or poster that can be distributed in schools.
9. Define the role of the Church during and after the Holocaust.
10. The Aryanization of Europe was a primary goal of the Third Reich. Students could research the diversity of students and faculty in their own schools. What cultures and religious beliefs are represented in their schools? How is difference and individualism honored and supported in a school environment? What are the difficulties of assimilation and retaining personal identification with your heritage? How is language diversity a growing presence in our schools?
11. Following World War II, a movement to deny the existence of the events of the

Holocaust began in the United States. Students could research this movement. What were its beginnings and how do revisionists still have a presence in the world today?

12. How is the German government recognizing its responsibility in the events of the Holocaust? How are the history books being written? What are reparations? Which countries paid reparations to survivors and their families? Which European governments are continuing to pay reparations?

13. The building of Holocaust memorial sites throughout Europe is controversial. Students should examine the artistic memorial sites and museums dedicated to the Holocaust in both Europe and the United States.

14. If a law in the United States is perceived as unjust, how do we as citizens change this law? What are the judicial and political procedures?

15. The Nazis used political propaganda to rally support for the Third Reich. How is propaganda used in contemporary society? Make a poster that promotes an idea that is relevant to students of your school (group or individual project).

16. Oral history assignment: Students should choose a person who participated in or lived during the time of World War II. The following are guidelines for how to conduct an interview:
   ▸ Be prepared for your interview. Do some research on the events of World War II. Research where, when, and why.
   ▸ Read several personal testimonies about the war.
   ▸ Prepare your questions before meeting your interviewee. Ask specific questions about place, time, and experience. As questions are answered, be sure to follow up with questions that specify additional detail in the answers.
   ▸ Have an audiotape or a video camera with you when you conduct your interview.
   ▸ Be prepared to take notes.
   ▸ Call your interviewee and arrange a meeting time and place. Schedule more than one session.
   ▸ Prepare an oral presentation for the class. Video and audiotape can be used to supplement your presentation.

17. Students could begin to read newspapers and periodicals about events around the world that deal with human rights, prejudice, ethnic wars, anti-Semitism, racism, and inequality. Over a two-week period, students should gather this information and be given time to work in small groups to create a poster on these issues. After the two weeks are completed, students should present their posters to their classmates. They should focus on the types of prejudice and injustice they discovered and its impact on the world community.

18. Students could prepare a display for their school on the Holocaust. The presentation could include the following:
   ▸ An overview of the Holocaust with maps and timelines
   ▸ Posters "advertising" appropriate novels and personal testimonies
   ▸ Art work created by students: drawings, painting, sculpture (see Art Chapter)
   ▸ Students could arrange for short talks in the library on what they have learned about the Holocaust

# A Select Bibliography _____

The following is a select list of books, both fiction and nonfiction, that I have used in my classroom and recommend for reading in a Holocaust curriculum.

   The list is certainly incomplete and reflects my personal choices in the literature as well as the books that are most commonly used in school programs across the country. For more complete bibliographies, I have listed several sources at the end of this list.

## Elementary

### Picture Books or Photography with Text

Abells, Chana Byers. *The Children We Remember*. New York: Greenwillow, 1983.

Adler, David. *The Number on My Grandfather's Arm*. New York: UAHC Press, 1987.

Bunting, Eve. *The Terrible Things*. Philadelphia: Jewish Publication Society, 1989.

Fluek, Toby. *Memories of My Life in a Polish Village*. New York: Knopf, 1990.

McDermott, Beverly Brodsky. *The Golem*. Philadelphia: J. P. Lippincott, 1976.

Ross, Lillian Hammer. *Buba Leah and Her Paper Children*. Philadelphia: The Jewish Publication Society, 1991.

## Grades 4 and Up

Increasing numbers of books are being published for grade levels four and up. These wonderful books provide both historical background and literary value in their fictionalized accounts of true-life events; it is difficult to classify these books separately from middle and upper school because of their use as important literary resources and historical perspectives for all grade levels.

### Historical, Historical Fiction, Personal Narrative

Adler, David. *We Remember the Holocaust*. New York: Bantam Books, 1989.

_____. *Child of the Warsaw Ghetto*. New York: Holiday House, 1995.

Anatoli, A. *Babi Yar: A Document in the Form of a Novel*. Cambridge, MA: Bentley Publishers, 1979.

Baer, Edith. *A Frost in the Night*. New York: Schocken Books, Inc., 1990.

Berenbaum, Michael. *The World Must Know: The History of the Holocaust As Told in the United States Holocaust Memorial Museum*. New York: Little, Brown & Co. (paper), 1993.

Bernheim, Mark. *Father of the Orphans: The Story of Januz Korzak*. New York: Dutton Children's Books, 1989.

Blatter, Janet, ed. *Art of the Holocaust*. New York: The Rutledge Press, 1981.

Boom, Corrie Ten. *The Hiding Place*. New York: Bantam Books, 1971.

Borowski, Tadeuz. *This Way for the Gas, Ladies and Gentlemen*. Translated by Barbara Veder. New York: Penguin Books, 1959.

Celan, Paul. *Poems of Paul Celan*. Translated by Michael Hamburger. New York: Persea Books, 1972.

Demetz, Hanna. *The House on Prague Street*. New York: St. Martin's Press, 1980.

*Documents on the Holocaust*. Yitzhak Arad, Yisrael Gutman, and Abraham Margaliot, eds. Israel: Yad Vashem, 1981.

Fink, Ida. *A Scrap of Time*. New York: Schocken Books, Inc., 1989.

Forché, Carolyn, ed. *Against Forgetting: Twentieth-Century Poetry of Witness*. New York: W. W. Norton & Co., 1993.

Frank, Anne. *Anne Frank: The Diary of a Young Girl*. New York: Doubleday, 1952.

Fremont, Helen. *After a Long Silence*. New York: A Delta Book, Dell Publishing, 1999.

Friedlander, Albert, ed. *Out of the Whirlwind*. New York: UAHC Press, 1999.

Fuchs, Elinore. *Plays of the Holocaust*. New York: Theater Communications Group, 1987.

Gotfryd, Bernard. *Anton, the Dove Fancier*. New York: Washington Square Press, 1990.

Haas, Gerda. *These I Do Remember*. Freeport, ME: The Cumberland Press, 1982.

Hegi, Ursula. *Stones from the River*. New York: Simon and Schuster, 1994.

*Images from the Holocaust: A Literature Anthology*. Jean E. Brown, Elaine C. Stephens, Janet E. Rubin, eds. National Textbook Company/Contemporary Publishing Group, 1997.

Hersh, Gizelle. *Gizelle, Save the Children*. Everett House, 1980.

Isaacman, Clara. *Clara's Story*. Philadelphia: The Jewish Publication Society of America, 1984.

Isaacson, Judith Magyar. *Seed of Sarah*. Urbana, Illinois: University of Illinois Press, 1991.

Innocenti, Roberto. *Rose Blanche*. New York: Harcourt, 1996.

Ippisch, Hanneke. *Sky: A True Story of Resistance During World War II*. New York: Simon & Schuster, 1996.

Kosinski, Jerzy. *The Painted Bird*. New York: Houghton Mifflin, 1965.

Lasky, Katherine. *The Night Journey*. New York: Viking, 1981.

Leitner, Isabella. *Fragments of Isabella*. New York: Dell, 1983.

Levi, Primo. *Survival in Auschwitz*. Orion, 1959.

Lowry, Lois. *Number the Stars*. New York: Dell, 1989.

Mochizuki, Ken. *Passage to Freedom: The Sugihara Story*. New York: Lee & Low Books, Inc., 1993.

Meltzer, Milton. *Never to Forget*. New York: Harper, 1976.

Miller, Arthur. *Incident At Vichy*. New York: Viking, 1965.

Moskin, Marietta. *I Am Rosemarie*. John Day, 1972.

Ozick, Cynthia. *The Shawl*. New York: Vintage Books, 1990.

Reiss, Johanna. *The Upstairs Room*. Harper, 1976.

Richter, Hans. *Friedrich*. New York: Viking, 1987.

Sachs, Nelly. *O The Chimneys*. Translated by Michael Hamburger. New York: Farrar, Straus and Giroux, 1967.

Schlink, Bernhard. *The Reader*. Translated by Carol Brown Janeway. New York: Vintage Press, 1995.

Scholl, Inge. *The White Rose*. Middletown, CT: Wesleyan University Press, 1983.

Seigal. Aranka. *Upon the Head of a Goat*. New York: Farrar, 1978.

_____. *Grace in the Wilderness: After the Liberation*. New York: Farrar Straus Group, 1985.

Spiegelman, Art. *Maus: A Survivor's Tale (Parts I & II)*. New York: Pantheon, 1986, 1991.

Stadtler, Bea. *The Holocaust: A History of Courage and Resistance*. West Orange, NJ: Behrman House, 1973.

Uris, Leon. *Exodus*. New York: Bantam Books Paperback Reissue, 1983.

_____. *Mila 18*. New York: Bantam Books Paperback Reissue, 1983.

Weinstein, Frida Scheps. *A Hidden Childhood*. New York: Farrar, Strauss, and Giroux, 1985.

Wiesel, Elie. *Night*. New York: Avon, 1972.

Yolen, Jane. *The Devil's Arithmetic*. New York: Viking, 1988.

## Resource Books

Please consult the Suggested Reading list at the conclusion of each chapter for additional sources for teacher research.

Anatoli, A. *Babi Yar: A Document in the Form of a Novel*. Cambridge, MA: Bentley Publishers, 1979.

Berenbaum, Michael and Abraham Peck, eds. *The Holocaust and History*. Bloomington and Indianapolis: Indiana University Press, 1998.

Blatter, Janet, ed. *Art of the Holocaust*. New York: The Rutledge Press, 1981.

Chartock, Roselle and Jack Spencer. *The Holocaust Years: Society on Trial*. New York: Bantam Books, 1978.

Dawidowicz, Lucy. *The War Against the Jews: 1933–1945*. New York: Bantam Books, 1986.

Des Pres, Terrence. *The Survivor: An Anatomy of Life in the Death Camps*. New York: Oxford University Press, 1976.

Green, Gerald, ed. *The Artists of Terezín*. Hawthorn Books, 1969.

Laqueur, Walter, ed. *The Holocaust Encyclopedia*. New Haven, CT: Yale University Press, 2001.

Langer, Lawrence L. *Holocaust Testimonies: The Ruins of Memory*. New Haven, CT: Yale University Press, 1991; New York: Oxford University Press, 1976.

_____. *The Holocaust and The Literary Imagination*. New Haven, CT: Yale University Press, 1975.

*Revolt Amid the Darkness. 1993 Days of Remembrance*. Washington, DC: United States Holocaust Memorial Museum, 1993.

Ringelblum, Emanuel and Joseph Kernish, eds. *Polish-Jewish Relations During the Second World War*. Evanston, IL: Northwestern University Press, 1992.

Stadlter, Bea. *The Holocaust: A History of Courage and Resistance*. West Orange, NJ: Behrman House, 1973.

Tec, Nechama. *When Light Pierced the Darkness. Christian Rescue of Jews in Nazi-Occupied Poland*. New York, NY: Oxford University Press, 1987.

Vishniac, Roman. *A Vanished World*. New York: Farrar and Strauss, 1983.

Wyman, David. *The Abandonment of the Jews*. New York: Pantheon, 1986.

## For More Extensive Bibliographies

*Days of Remembrance 1992, Revolt Amid the Darkness 1993.* Washington, DC: United States Holocaust Memorial Museum.

*The Spirit That Moves Us,* Volumes I & II, Holocaust Human Rights Center of Maine. Gardiner, ME: Tilbury House, Publishers.

*Facing History and Ourselves Resource Book,* Facing History and Ourselves National Foundation, Inc.

## Videography

*Au Revoir Les Enfant,* Louis Malle, France

*Daring to Resist: Three Women Face the Holocaust,* Women Make Movies, Martha Lubell Productions

*Dark Lullabies,* DLI & National Film Board of Canada

*Elie Wiesel: Nobel Prize Series,* IMG Educators/Nobel Foundation

*Judgment at Nuremburg,* Stanley Kramer, Abby Mann

*Lodz Ghetto,* The Jewish Heritage Project 158

*Night and Fog,* Alain Resnais, Argos, Jean Cayrol

*Schindler's List,* Steven Spielberg

*Seed of Sarah,* The Cinema Guild

*Shoah,* Claude Lanzmann

*The Courage to Care,* United Way

*The Last Days,* Steven Spielberg

*The White Rose,* Michael Verhoeven, Social Studies School Services

*Triumph of the Will,* Leni Riefenstahl

*Wannsee Conference,* Infafilm, GmbH, Munich, Germany

*Warsaw Ghetto,* BBC TV

## CD-ROMs

*Anne Frank House: the Complete Story of Anne Frank, the Annex, and Those in Hiding,* Cinegram

*Eclipse of Humanity: The History of the Shoah,* Yad Vashem

*Lest We Forget: A History of the Holocaust,* Logos Research Systems

*My Brother's Keeper,* Clearvue

*Return to Life: The Story of the Holocaust Survivors,* Yad Vashem

*Stories from the Warsaw Ghetto: Voices From the Past,* Montparnasse

*Survivors: Testimonies of the Holocaust, Survivors of the Shoah,* Visual History Foundation

*World War II: Global Conflict and World War II: Sources and Analysis,* two CD-ROMs from Mentorom

## About the Holocaust Human Rights Center of Maine

The Holocaust Human Rights Center of Maine (HHRC) grew out of a seminar, "Teaching About the Nazi Holocaust in Maine Schools," held at Bowdoin College in 1984. The participants found the seminar to be a powerful and compelling commentary on the fragility of democracy. Under the leadership of Gerda Haas, a Holocaust survivor and the author of books about the Holocaust, the Holocaust Human Rights Center of Maine was incorporated in May 1985 and declared its purpose: "To foster public education about the Holocaust and issues of human rights that grow out of reflection on that historic event."

The Center's goal is to teach the lessons that can be learned from the Holocaust, about what can happen when basic human rights are destroyed. Through education, the Center works to reduce prejudice and to create an environment of tolerance, acceptance, and well-being among all people.

The Center has produced *Maine Survivors Remember the Holocaust*, an Emmy-nominated documentary that was released nationally, and, with Tilbury House, Publishers, published *The Spirit That Moves Us, Volume I: A Literature-Based Resource Guide, Teaching about Diversity, Prejudice, Human Rights, and the Holocaust*, for teachers of Grades K–4, and *The Spirit That Moves Us, Volume II: A Literature-Based Resource Guide, Teaching about the Holocuast and Human Rights*, for teachers of Grades 5–8. The Center sponsors week-long summer seminars for educators, Diversity Leadership Institutes for teenagers, and Days of Remembrance commemorations.

Holocaust Human Rights Center of Maine
PO Box 4645
Augusta, ME 04330
Phone/Fax 207-993-2620
www.hhrc.org

## About Tilbury House, Publishers

Tilbury House is a small, independent publisher in Maine, specializing in children's books about cultural diversity, nature, or environmental issues; teacher's guides; and adult non-fiction about Maine and New England. Please visit our web site at www.tilburyhouse.com, or call 800-582-1899 for a free catalog.

Tilbury House, Publishers
2 Mechanic Street
Gardiner, ME 04345
800–582–1899/Fax 207-582-8227
www.tilburyhouse.com